# BORDERLINES

The Essential Guide to Understanding and Living with Complex Borderline Personality Disorder. Know Yourself. Love Yourself. And Let Others Love You

## SIENA DA SILVA

# CONTENTS

# ACKNOWLEDGMENTS

## I am grateful to:

*The Sassy Miss Ali*

*Alysha Myers...Go Team!*

*Cover Design: Radu_Muresan*

*www.facebook.com/borderlinesarah92*

*My Teachers: CM & RM*

# ABOUT THE AUTHOR

I have practiced as a specialist in Children and Family Law for over 20 years. On the job, I have witnessed the good, the bad, and the ugly of human behavior and closely studied the psychological analyses of the individuals in my investigations. I have experienced firsthand how difficult life can be for the sufferers of untreated mental disorders and their loved ones. I write with a passion for understanding the human psyche ,to give back to the community by sharing my knowledge and experience regarding this subject. I set up The Psychology School Publishing with the aim of creating accessible, read-able, and understandable literature.

# INTRODUCTION: YOU ARE NOT ALONE

A person walking on the sidewalk stumbled and almost fell. Here's how their internal monologue went: "Oh, jeez. That was so embarrassing. How many people saw that? Are they all looking at me or am I just imagining it? I'm so dumb. I can't even walk right. I should never leave the house ever again. That's it, I'm cancelling all my plans and going straight home."

This kind of reaction may be very familiar to you and would be very typical of someone with Borderline Personality Disorder (Also known as Emotionally Unstable Personality Disorder). Chances are they suspect something's wrong with them too and their friends and family have picked up on it. It is common for people with borderline personality disorder (BPD) to be severely afflicted by what are seemingly trivial events. They can swing from being perfectly alright one second to a shattered resolve and extreme self-loathing the next.

People suffering from BPD experience emotions on an incredibly nuclear level. That goes to say for both positive and negative emotions. When they feel happy, they can bubble up with contagiously positive energy. When they feel love, it can be to an extraordinary extent such that they are brimming with it. On the other hand, negative emotions – including anger, jealousy, hatred, and sadness – can feel like the end of the world. It can be hard to contain the fire of those emotions, which can make you prone to lashing out. This is known as *emotional lability*, which is characterized by unstable mood, intense mood swings, and strong emotional reactions to stressors. During these highs and lows, people close to you will find it challenging to be around you. It can feel like they are "walking on eggshells" around their loved one struggling with BPD. The smallest gesture, albeit misinterpreted, a slight change in tone of voice, or feeling insulted by something said can cause a strong reaction from the person suffering.(More about TRIGGERS and SPLITTING later).

BPD can manifest itself as low confidence and self-worth. It can make you question who you are and distort your sense of self. One minute, you feel comfortable in your own skin and happy with the way you look, and the next, you can hate your-self for merely existing, or even view yourself as a terrible person.

Tumultuous, unstable relationships are common amongst people with BPD. You may find yourself swinging between idealizing people and growing to intensely dislike them within short periods. There's a constant fear of ABANDONMENT that may denote an insecure attachment style. You feel compelled to actively avoid abandonment and the mere thought of being rejected can trigger an intense bout of anxiety. You start to worry that you're the problem but you cannot shake some of the worst fears of your loved ones leaving you.

Fear and uncertainty are natural emotional responses to feeling threatened by things we cannot comprehend. Fear can hamper the brain's ability to process the information in front of us, disrupt emotional regulation, and the ability to read non-verbal cues. This impacts our capability to make decisions and control our impulses, therefore, influencing our behavior.

Emotional lability in people with BPD can amplify their fear response. You pass situations through filters you have developed in your mind to protect yourself from judgment. Therefore, you might find yourself lashing out, being verbally or physically abusive, internalizing, or developing grudges over mere speculations or actual hostilities and conflicts. You act up out of fear.

Feelings can seep into the rational parts of anyone's brain. It's only human. However, what comes with feeling so intensely in BPD is black and white thinking, also known as "splitting". It can jeopardize the quality of your life and your relationships.

Logic is out the window and the assumptions kick in. Thoughts like "My professor suggested an improvement in my work, therefore, I know nothing about my course," or "My partner didn't text me first today. He must be seeing someone else" occur. Splitting is not a conscious choice for the one struggling with BPD. It is usually brought on by a *trigger*, meaning an external event or internal process such as a memory or thought that suddenly worsens symptoms.

Things can either only be perfect or a total disaster. The grey area rarely exists. These splitting episodes can lead to having thoughts of self-harm due to catastrophic thinking. Hurting oneself or engaging in self-harm and suicidal tendencies is as low as it can get for anyone struggling with mental illness. It's a critical symptom that requires immediate medical attention. It's not unusual to see a BPD sufferer with bandaged wrists, arms, and thighs from where they have taken to cutting to relieve their pain, temporarily.

It is unfortunate that not only is Borderline Personality Disorder under-recognised but it is also significantly challenging for mental health professionals to diagnose and treat, owing to the complexity of its traits and overlapping of its symptoms with other mental health conditions like bipolar disorder and PTSD.

The ongoing social stigma surrounding BPD does not help those who suffer from it. The narrative some misinformed people paint of those struggling with borderline personality disorder can be rather malicious. You are not as flawed or unlovable as you think you are. You are merely struggling and you have the right to seek help and live your life just as well as others do.

Please know that you are not alone. Thousands of others have been in this dark and confusing place. Strange new places need getting used to if you're going to be there for a long time. Eventually, you will gain familiarity with your surroundings and be able to draw out maps around the obstacles. Especially if life has not been very kind to you and it feels like you have had to steer your ship through a turbulent sea, struggling to stay afloat in all its aspects; the added weight of mental illness can take a toll on you.

We know that BPD exists and is very difficult to live with. However, many people don't quite know what to do about it. Don't leave your condition untreated. Don't abandon yourself for there is life for you to live and people to love. You deserve to feel heard, understood, and helped. It's high time you learned about the reasons behind why you are the way you are, how you are unique, and what you can do to pave a path to a healthier life − a life that is as normal as it can get for someone living with BPD. You have my word, there *is* help out there. In this book, I will talk you through your journey to understanding what borderline personality disorder is, and what you can do to make your life easier and be able to breathe better.

This book covers numerous fundamentals of the types of personality disorders and their characteristics, mainly dealing with BPD. We will go over its causes and treatment options, and discuss misconceptions. You will understand the reasons behind your self-destructive behavior and thought patterns to help give you clarity. Last but not least, you will learn to take care of yourself.

You would benefit from knowing that an example of a gold-standard treatment option many people with BPD benefit from is Dialectical Behavior Therapy. The results of a study of psychotherapy for people with BPD found that DBT is very helpful. Effects included a decrease in inappropriate anger, a reduction in self–harm, and an improvement in general functioning. (Stoffers-Winterling, 2012)

BPD is an extremely complex and excruciating illness that can hurt the one who's suffering from it as well as their loved ones. It is important to disassemble the stigma and create more awareness of the recovery steps that people with BPD can take towards improvement and self-growth. To help you gain a better understanding of a subject that is so complicated at the first glance is something I intend to achieve through my writing.

Start this read with a little compassion for yourself. I hope this book can be some solace for you amidst the noise in your head.

*Disclaimer: Do not use the information from this book to self-diagnose. Only a trained mental health professional is qualified to diagnose mental illness.*

# 1

# SO, YOU THINK YOU HAVE A PERSONALITY DISORDER?

## Understanding what a personality disorder is and its types

This chapter will help you learn more about personality disorders in general. You will learn about the characteristics of the disorders and what they look like. More importantly, you will gain insight into terms and psychological patterns that will help you understand your condition better, especially since the symptoms can overlap. You'll start to see if you can recognize yourself.

The line between psychology and psychiatry is blurred. Their terms are often used synonymously, even incorrectly, but there are clear differences between the two fields.

Psychology is the study or the science of how the mind works and how it is linked to behavior. It focuses on personality. The word 'psychology' is derived from a Greek word: 'psyche' which means the mind, soul, or spirit and 'logos' which means discourse or 'to study'. It also comes from the Latin that describes "the study of the soul".

It applies many different methods to search for answers and the schools of thought it explores.

The brain is, in a way, a universe in itself. Humans constantly venture to understand the mind and its complexity. We take leaps to understand ourselves and each discovery made, every successful definition and explanation we can come up with brings us closer to making sense of why we are the way we are.

As a person with BPD, you must be asking yourself, "Why am I acting this way even when I don't want to?"

Well, to answer that, one of the main questions psychology asks, which is the one that concerns us in this book, is "What is mental illness and what can we do about it?" We discuss the work of psychologists in the treatment of mental health disorders further in chapter 2.

Psychology overlaps with psychiatry when it comes to treating mental illnesses. Psychiatry is a medical speciality that focuses on diagnosing and treating mental, emotional, or behavioral illnesses. Psychiatrists are medical doctors that can prescribe medication after proper assessment of the patient.

The two fields overlap as they both involve the treatment and study of dysfunctional human behaviors, mental health conditions and emotional wellbeing. In future treatment, you may see either a psychologist or a psychiatrist or both.

Personality is determined by various factors like a person's genes, the environment they have grown up and lived in, and the experiences they have had that shape their habits. Everyone has a personality that is unique to them. It's what makes us all different from each other. It's possible to share sets of personality traits that make us quite similar as well. A personality trait is an internal characteristic that reflects a person's pattern of thoughts, behaviors, feelings, and habits. This characteristic generally persists and isn't changeable. It can describe how a person would act in different situations e.g. someone that scores low on a specific trait like 'Extroversion' is likely to prefer indoor activities and avoid loud parties when it comes to spending time with friends.

Let's start breaking down personality disorders.

## WHAT ARE PERSONALITY DISORDERS?

A personality disorder makes a person feel, think, behave, and act differently from normal people. They deviate from what's socially acceptable, causing distress and problems with functioning in daily life. A person with mental illness can be known as *neurodivergent* or *neurodiverse*, meaning someone that is far more different than the normal majority in mental processes and ways of thinking.

Personality disorders can be grouped into 10 specific mental health disorders.

A person suffering from a personality disorder has disruptive patterns of thinking, behavior, and mood relative to others. People with a mental health condition like this will rarely realize the consequences that their thoughts and behaviors can have or how problematic they can be.

To understand what a personality disorder is, we will briefly discuss psychological disorders and how they are grouped in general. There are two groups of psychological disorders: ego-dystonic and ego-syntonic.

*Ego Dystonic* people are aware they have a problem and tend to be concerned with their symptoms. Their beliefs, thoughts about themselves, and behaviors go against the way they see themselves and do not feed their ego. In stressful situations, they react by turning inwards to alter their thinking process and desire ways to change themselves.

For example, a person with OCD is aware their disorder takes a toll on them and they are not happy with it. Imagine someone with OCD who feels compelled to meticulously scrub their hands clean with soap for 2 minutes followed by rinsing for another 2 minutes. They are aware of how much time this takes out and how sore and wrinkled their fingers are afterward, but they cannot help themselves. Similarly, every night, the same person feels they need to check the lock exactly 4 times by repeatedly locking, unlocking, then opening, and closing the door to lock it again. Not following their routine will distress them far more.

Some disorders are more complex, such as *ego-syntonic disorders*. The person experiencing them doesn't always think they have a problem and sometimes believes that it is everyone else that is flawed and in the wrong. Their beliefs, feelings, and behavior cater to the way they see themselves and feed their ego. In distress, they will turn outwards, blame the circumstance or others around them, and may refuse to acknowledge any problem within themselves.

Personality disorders come under this category. People with ego syntonic disorders rarely recognize that they need to get diagnosed or treated, let alone accept that they have a problem. They simply are not aware of what's wrong with themselves.

For example, a BPD sufferer imagines their partner leaving them for someone else. The person with BPD starts to blame their partner for no longer loving them whilst in a fit of rage, gets up, and storms off, leaving them in a state of confusion.

Instead of addressing their thoughts and wondering why they imagined such a case with their partner, the sufferer acted out and blamed the other person as a way to cope with their fear of abandonment. In reading this book, however, you are different and are looking for answers and understanding.

Psychological disorders are characterized by stubborn, disruptive, and lasting behavior patterns that impair social and other functioning - whether the sufferer recognizes it or not. They are believed to be chronic syndromes that create ripples of problems in life that can last.

## TYPES OF PERSONALITY DISORDERS

It is useful to briefly look at all PDs so that you understand that there can be an overlap in traits between them. You may also see more of yourself in a PD other than BPD?

Personality disorders can be categorized by the 'DSM-5' into three groups known as clusters A, B, and C. The 'DSM-5' means the fifth edition of the Diagnostic and Statistical Manual of Mental Disorders. It is one of the main tools used by mental health professionals when evaluating or diagnosing mental disorders in patients.

It's important to note that it does not include treatments for mental disorders, but simply classifies disorders, describes their potential causes and presentations.

### Cluster A personality disorders

People with cluster A personality disorder have a difficult time relating to other people. They can be thought to have odd or eccentric ways of thinking and behaving.

### *Paranoid personality disorder*

This disorder is marked by *paranoia* - which is constant distrust and suspicion of others without any good reason. It means people with paranoia are always under the impression that others are out to hurt them, that others will betray their trust or take advantage of them.

They have difficulty opening up to loved ones which prevents them from forming sustainable, close relationships with family members, workplace colleagues, or friends. People that struggle with paranoia are also likely to hold grudges or be rather unforgiving towards those they suspect. They aren't the type to give others a second chance. Their skepticism and avoidant behavior function to help them feel safe.

### Schizoid personality disorder

People with schizoid personality disorder appear detached and generally uninterested in all relationships and social inter- actions. To an outsider, they might seem lonely and detached from their surroundings as well as others.

People with schizoid cases aren't very determined to make friends or get involved in relationships. They either lack the social skills to put themselves out there or they just prefer their own company; have a general dislike of growing close to others, even family.

### Schizotypal personality disorder

In schizotypal disorder, the person displays a pattern of discomfort and reluctance around forming close relationships.

They can have a superstitious or distorted perception of real- ity. Their behavior, thoughts, and beliefs are rather unusual or 'a bit weird' and that can set them apart from others. This refers to interpersonal 'awkwardness'. They especially worry around people that do not share the same beliefs as them so they're likely to be withdrawn at times and avoid socializing to protect themselves from being judged.

What sets schizotypal apart from schizoid is that schizotypal personality disorder is marked by paranoia. Additionally, unlike individuals with schizoid disorder who don't like to socialize, those with schizotypal personality disorder may crave close relationships but their symptoms get in the way of connecting with others.

## Cluster B personality disorders

Cluster B personality disorder types are based on those who find it difficult to control their emotions. People with cluster B personality disorder(s) are viewed as dramatic, overemotional, unpredictable, and impulsive.

### *Borderline personality disorder*

BPD falls within Cluster B. People with BPD present with poor self-image, fear of abandonment, impulsivity, and dramatic mood swings. This set of dysfunction results in relationship difficulties and trouble holding down a job or career. BPD is currently one of the most researched and studied personality disorders which is good news for sufferers going forward as therapies and treatments should improve as should the broader understanding of the population in general.

From the name, it sounds like the sufferer is almost on the normal side of the spectrum, but not completely abnormal either. However, that is not the case.

BPD patients are used to getting their psychological needs such as desires for love and validation met by using dysfunctional and problematic behaviors such as lashing out, outbursts of rage and anger, and self-injury.

At a point in time, clinicians even misinterpreted BPD patients as 'attention-seeking', 'difficult', or 'melodramatic' but fortunately, that has changed.

Records show that the population with a BPD diagnosis can range from 2-7%. Refer to chapter 2 for a deep dive into the details of BPD.

### *Antisocial personality disorder* (also known as "sociopathy")

People with an antisocial personality disorder don't follow social norms and etiquette, or they are simply not aware of them. They generally lack respect for others and are unable to take responsibility for their actions, having the impression of 'rule-breakers'. Most lie, act impulsively or show aggression, and are likely to indulge excessively in drugs and alcohol. Their lifestyle and lack of morality often make them unfit to participate functionally in society.

### *Histrionic personality disorder*

The term 'histrionic' comes from the Latin word for "actor". It means 'theatrical' or 'overly dramatic'.

Although this personality disorder is counted in the DSM-5 as an official diagnosis, many mental health professionals share the view that it is ambiguous, extremely stigmatizing and mostly, sexist. It's important to know about the context, so let's briefly look at the history of how this diagnosis came about.

The disorder was also known as a hysterical personality disorder, marked by *hysteria*. 'Hysteria' is derived from the ancient Greek word "hystera," which means the 'uterus or womb' and it was used by Egyptians in 1900 B.C. to record behavioral abnormalities in women. Hysteria was known as a "woman's disease" and it was used exclusively to label women who exhibited any symptoms from a wide range that includes paralysis, epilepsy, emotional or mental abnormalities, etc.

This personality disorder is marked by intense, fluctuating emotions and a warped self-image. People with this condition have an immense desire for external validation. It is thought that they will go to lengths to set themselves apart from others to seek attention typically by using physical appearance. Other behaviors include acting up or being impulsive, being sexually provocative and engaging in dangerous or even suicidal behaviors to gain attention.

### Narcissistic personality disorder

Narcissists feel difficult to be around, especially if someone doesn't have strong boundaries and isn't as informed on how to spot narcissistic traits. People may describe narcissists as 'selfish', 'manipulative' or 'patronizing', who act as if they're know-it-alls.

People with this disorder can show a lack of empathy for others and a grandiose sense of self-importance and entitlement, hence they are considered 'selfish' by most. They may tend to exploit others without feeling any guilt or shame, hence considered to be 'manipulative'.

In short, this disorder is characterized by a pattern of self-perceived superiority and grandiosity, expectations of high praise and admiration from others.

## Cluster C personality disorders

These can involve extreme anxiety and fear, lack of self-esteem, and general avoidance of meeting new people.

### Avoidant personality disorder

People suffering from this condition struggle with feelings of inadequacy and self-doubt. They are highly sensitive and fear being judged by others so they tend to struggle in growing close to and connecting with others initially. They may come off as extremely shy, timid or reserved. Mostly, they are highly sensitive to criticism or disapproval from others so they'll avoid situations that hold any possibility of failure, which means a lack of work, school or social life.

### Dependent personality disorder

'Dependent' being the opposite of 'avoidant', this disorder is characterized by an overwhelming string of thoughts and feelings related to needing others that can impact the sufferer's daily life and relationships.

Individuals that struggle with this personality disorder will hand others the driving stick to their life and want to let others take responsibility for their life. They are extremely afraid of losing others' support or being left alone. In addition, they struggle with low self-confidence and see others as more capable compared to themselves.

They will put aside themselves if necessary to avoid abandonment, owing to their strong people-pleasing trait. Constantly seeking reassurance and advice from others, they strongly lack the ability of taking care of themselves and in making their own decisions.

### Obsessive-Compulsive personality disorder (OCPD)

This personality disorder is not the same as obsessive-compulsive disorder (OCD), which is related more to the form of behavior rather than a type of personality, specifically ego-dystonic behavior (we discussed ego-dystonic vs. ego-syntonic near the start of this chapter). On the other hand,

OCPD relates more to ego-syntonic behavior, meaning it is consistent with the person's own beliefs and attitudes.

Although it is similar to OCD in the way that it does involve the need for control, problems with perfectionism, and difficulty in shifting mindsets, people with OCPD strongly believe that their way of doing things is the correct and the only way to do them. They may have a critical, holier-than-thou attitude in most situations.

## BPD and co-morbidities

*Co-morbidity* means the presence of two or more diseases at the same time in a person.

It is common to have more than one mental health condition at the same time in people with BPD, such as depression and anxiety. Therefore, comorbidities are more common in people with BPD. Studies show that 96% of patients with BPD have a mood disorder during their life, and lifetime depression is reported at 71% to 83%. Anxiety disorders are also common with the following rates: 88% of patients have an anxiety disorder, 34% to 48% have panic disorder, and 47% to 56% have PTSD. Alcohol and substance abuse or dependence are reported by 50% to 65%; eating disorders affect 7% to 26% over a lifetime. (Biskin & Paris, 2013)

Getting the right diagnosis is difficult because symptoms of different mental health disorders can overlap.

While clinicians can identify if a patient checks all the boxes for signs and symptoms of a personality disorder, details of the condition can be difficult to outline.

Recognizing and diagnosing BPD is more challenging compared to anxiety or depression.

Mental illnesses are generally difficult to diagnose because, firstly, there is no fixed litmus or medical test or lab work that can be carried out to screen and confirm them. Secondly, many symptoms and manifestations overlap and mimic each other in different mental disorders e.g., frequent or intense mood swings are common in both BPD as well as bipolar disorder.

Every case is different as people are shaped uniquely by separate experiences from growing up in different environments and circumstances. Mental health professionals need to understand and treat every patient individually, starting by focusing on their lifestyle and thought patterns and understanding the context of their symptoms. By building context, symptoms can be identified much more easily. For example, one patient can report low moods and a lack of interest for a longer duration than someone else.

Even clinicians are prone to making the wrong diagnosis, which does not help the recovery or treatment process and can even exacerbate the sufferer's condition and the symptoms of BPD. A good mental health professional would care more about treating symptoms rather than the disease in the bigger picture.

You need to be aware of the common co-morbidities to ensure you have the correct diagnosis. So you can help yourself or your loved one in finding the help they need. When BPD occurs with another mental health condition e.g., anxiety disorder, both conditions should be treated at the same time.

Psychotic, affective, and anxiety disorders frequently coexist. BPD patients with co-morbidities can be challenging to treat, requiring the psychiatrist's or psychologist's utmost attention because they pose a high risk for suicidal tendencies. It also means a poorer quality of functioning and mental processes as compared to having a single condition, a greater chance of relapse, and a less positive response to treatment. Co-morbid personality disorders have increased suicide risk ,more than mood and substance use disorders.

Common co-morbidities for those with BPD are listed below. You may already have a diagnosis of one or more of these. They are further explained in the next chapter as *differential diagnoses* - the clinician looks at all the possible diseases that can explain your systems to rule out the incorrect one, make the diagnosis and form a treatment plan.

- *Substance abuse disorder*
- *Bipolar disorder*

- *Anxiety disorders*
- *Major Depressive Disorder (MDD)*
- *Post-Traumatic Stress Disorder (PTSD)*

# 2

# "WHAT'S WRONG WITH ME?"

## Where and who to go to for diagnosis and help

Personality disorders are long-term, dysfunctional, and abnormal behavior patterns that are difficult to change and lead to social issues. People struggling with a personality disorder, especially those without a diagnosis, easily feel misunderstood by those around them, and they are not wrong for feeling the way they do.

It takes a lot of guts to accept that you do have a problem. Second, it takes a lot of patience, dedication to understanding yourself, time, and effort to work on addressing the problems you do have.

Many people with BPD are not aware that they have it. They are not able to stop and realize how unhealthy their behavior is and how it affects others. There is no overnight cure for BPD. But, we are moving forward in research and science at every given moment. We have come to learn a lot about BPD as well and have improved in diagnosing and treating it.

Borderline Personality Disorder is just one of the 10 personality disorders. This is just an example of a rare case, but, a person can have some traits of more than one personality disorder e.g., they can share traits of both paranoid personality disorder as well as BPD but not have the complete symptoms to qualify for a diagnosis of the full form of either of them at the same time. It also means that a person can be diagnosed with more than just one personality disorder.

Getting a diagnosis is not easy at all, but it is worth the work if it means you can help yourself and those who know you. For that, you will need to turn to mental health professionals - psychologists and psychiatrists. However, you may first need to see your general doctor who can then make arrangements for you to see someone more specialized, for assessment and treatment. Some psychologists and psychiatrists are ok with being approached directly but if you have a good relationship with your GP they may be the best person to speak to first of all and can pass on your full medical history. To some extent, it may depend on the country you live in.

Psychologists also work as therapists: trained mental health professionals who provide what is called "talking therapy" to patients with mental illness. Their field of expertise involves the study of personality, the set of unique traits, patterns of thoughts, and behavior that make up a person.

Seeing a therapist will help you learn healthy ways to handle the challenges of mental illnesses like BPD, depression and bipolar disorder.

If you are to see a psychiatrist, they will be better able to treat your symptoms by careful assessment of your case and then prescribing the right medication, if appropriate, and particularly if they find you also have a mental illness, such as depression, as well. Presently, it is understood that there are no medications solely for BPD but this is an area of continued research.

Working towards a diagnosis can involve seeing multiple practitioners. It's a process. People with BPD do not get along very well with people whom they cannot see as allies. As much as care providers for BPD only mean well, the sufferers may perceive suggestions of improvement and addressing their problem areas as harsh judgment and criticism. This is why you need to try to be on board with your doctor or counselor and share compatibility with and, even more, understand that the purpose of seeing them is to improve your quality of life. If you don't feel comfortable with a health professional or therapist, you shouldn't be afraid to ask to see someone else. This is a vital relationship for you so it is essential it works for you and you can trust in that relationship.

## GETTING A DIAGNOSIS

The basic requirement for a diagnosis of BPD is to have at least 5 verified traits. The Diagnostic and Statistical Manual of Mental Disorders (DSM) is the official source of information used to diagnose psychiatric disorders, including BPD. For each condition or disorder, it lists the symptoms and specifies how many symptoms are needed, along with their severity, to guarantee a diagnosis.

BPD is indicated by at least 5 or more of the following 9:

1. Difficulty controlling emotions in day-to-day events (e.g. anxiety, episodic sadness, or irritability lasting a few hours or sometimes more than a few days)
2. Making frantic efforts to avoid abandonment (even if it's imagined)
3. Feelings of emptiness
4. Lack of identity with a distorted self-image and unsure sense of self
5. Impulsive, potentially self-damaging behavior in at least two areas e.g. spending, substance abuse, binge eating,risky sexual encounters, etc
6. Poor anger management including frequent outbursts of rage or difficulty controlling anger, recurrent fights or arguments, strong reactions.
7. A pattern of unstable relationships. Frequently having a change of mind between idealizing and devaluing the person known as *splitting.*

8. *Paranoid ideation* or *dissociative* symptoms-dissociation.

9. Self-injury, suicidal tendencies, threats of committing suicide or actual attempts to end life.

It is possible to suffer from more than one mental health condition in addition to BPD. This is important for mental health practitioners to bear in mind when treating a patient with BPD or someone suspected of having BPD. One of the reasons why getting the right diagnosis is difficult is because the symptoms of different mental health disorders can overlap. Most BPD sufferers have co-morbid conditions. It can seem like several mental health disorders wrapped into one big illness.

Knowing all the possibilities and issues that can co-exist will increase awareness of the different needs to account for when assessing a person's life, personality, thoughts, and behavior patterns.

As mentioned in the previous chapter, comorbidity means the presence of more than one condition or disease in the sufferer. These co-morbidities need to be understood differently, in addition to BPD, to paint the bigger picture. Depressive or anxious symptoms and tendencies are a part of BPD. They are driven by BPD and are not standalone. However, you may also be diagnosed with depression or an anxiety disorder.

Therefore, your mental health provider would come up with what is called *differential diagnoses*, which is listing all the possible conditions or diseases that could be causing your symptoms and fit the description of your case. They do not make up the final diagnosis, of course. But they certainly help work towards building the correct one eventually. This is how the problem of overlapping symptoms between conditions is dealt with. For example, medication and cognitive behavioral therapy that is intended to treat depression will not have a significant impact on BPD itself. The mood fluctuations, impulsivity, and feelings of emptiness that characterize BPD will still be there unless treated with focus.

It is helpful to be well-informed about the different disorders that can overlap with BPD to help you have a better understanding of your condition.

## CO-MORBIDITIES EXPLAINED

### Substance use disorder

Substance use disorder is diagnosed when a person's recurrent use of drugs or alcohol leads to dysfunction and noticeable distress in their daily life.

It is possible to be co-morbid with substance use disorder for BPD patients due to the impulsivity trait. Between 14 and 72 percent of people with BPD will also have a substance use disorder. (Sansone, 2011). What distinguishes persons with BPD is that they have to demonstrate impulsivity in other areas such as spending, sex, binge eating, for example.

## Bipolar disorder

The person with bipolar disorder fluctuates drastically between low (depressive) and high (hypomanic/manic) moods and has difficulty managing their emotions. They also struggle with impulsivity. Sounds pretty similar to BPD.

These are the common symptoms shared by BPD as well, which means that people with bipolar disorder and those with BPD will have an equally challenging time reaching the right diagnosis.

What helps rule out bipolar disorder is knowing that people with BPD experience more social problems like rocky relationships, extreme fear of abandonment, and trust issues. They can quickly grow from having a high regard for someone to holding a grudge against them. Therefore, as mentioned previously, a mental health professional needs to observe and understand the person's thought patterns, relationships, and the way they see themselves. Quite similar to getting acquainted with someone in order to get to know them better.

## Anxiety disorders

Anxiety disorder is a group of illnesses characterized by intense fear and worry that can feel out of control and long-lasting.

Panic disorder is characterized by episodes of panic attacks that don't exactly have any triggers. A panic attack sort of makes you feel like you're dying and can be very scary.

One of the symptoms of BPD is anxiety. Between 75 and 90 percent of people with BPD meet the criteria for at least one type of anxiety disorder, such as social anxiety disorder and panic disorder.

The difference between BPD and anxiety disorder is that in anxiety disorder symptoms occur more frequently and last longer, for at least six months. It can be very confusing.

## Major Depressive Disorder (MDD)

Major depressive disorder (MDD) has been found to occur in 83 percent of individuals with BPD. Symptoms of depression are common in BPD which, again, means making an accurate diagnosis difficult since two diseases are co-occurring with symptoms that already overlap.

You need to be sure that the diagnosis between BPD and MDD is correct because treatment of MDD does not mean remission of BPD. Therefore, BPD is not to be confused with affective (mood) disorders like depression.

Symptoms of depression in BPD can be situational or brief. They are believed to be related to social problems such as unstable relationships or after a fight with a partner where you are left feeling hurt or rejected.

Depressive symptoms in BPD may also be manifestations of feelings that are not expressed in healthy ways such as expressions of anger, hatred, helplessness, hurt, or disappointment. Borderlines may communicate how unhappy they are about a person or situation in a rather awkward or dysfunctional way. In such a case, they can only help themselves by asking, "What is causing me to feel this way? Where is the hurt coming from? What can I do about it?" They can be guided to address their problem in more adaptive or well-suited ways.

## Post-Traumatic Stress Disorder (PTSD)

PTSD is a mental health condition that occurs in people who have witnessed or gone through a difficult, shocking, and disturbing traumatic event e.g. physical or emotional abuse, sexual assault, car accident, or war. This can ,of course, be the same for Borderlines.

Trauma from abuse or neglect can reshape and rewire a person's personality in a damaged way. Even when a person has not necessarily grown up in a difficult environment, some are shown to have greater sensitivity to abuse or trauma by genetic predisposition. Studies show that early childhood trauma can alter the brain and increase the chances of someone developing BPD.

However, a person with BPD can have experienced trauma but if they do not show symptoms of PTSD, they do not meet the criteria for a PTSD diagnosis. Conversely, the trauma suffered may mean someone has both BPD and PTSD, and both need different treatment.

## Stigma

There's a stigma - a stereotype that causes someone to think less of the person in question - that surrounds BPD and mental illness in general. Stigma is an issue that needs to be urgently dealt with because it makes getting effective treatment difficult. BPD behaviors admittedly are confusing, unpredictable, and sometimes even manipulative.

Living with a mental illness is already difficult enough but having to deal with negative assumptions from misinformed people is just unfair. Many patients with BPD struggle with internalized stigma as well. Internalized stigma is high levels of self-stigma that come from a place of shame and unhappiness due to society and prejudice. This can often deter someone from getting the treatment they need.

Patients that have been diagnosed with BPD often feel embarrassed. They feel as though they have been labeled with a diagnosis that sets them apart, attracts negative assumptions and repels people from them in general. Granted, there is discrimination against people with BPD. Some mental health providers that are less experienced even claim that BPD is not treatable as patients can resist their efforts to provide treatment. Some may even ignore the signs which can lead to misdiagnosis. To achieve treatment success, it's best if your mental health provider has experience treating BPD and keeps an open mind while treating you.

You and your mental health provider need to connect and have compatibility to identify your inner thoughts, behaviors, and beliefs to help you replace impulses with healthy coping mechanisms that deal with your fears. It will keep you motivated and steady in therapy and treatment. You will be more willing and open to learning new good habits and unlearning the bad ones.

Don't let stigma demotivate you or make you feel ashamed. Rather, learn as much as you can about your diagnosis and share facts about it. Reading this book is a very positive first step. Understanding something complex makes it less scary and daunting.

BPD has a good prognosis, which means effective treatment following a diagnosis: a positive outcome. It's a long journey and you will face challenges along the way. It is okay to need encouragement and reassurance throughout the process. Hold on to hope and your loved ones.

Putting aside the stigma and accepting your diagnosis will help you deepen your understanding and confront the challenges of BPD. You will set foot on a hopeful path leading you to a healthier, happier life.

## WE ALL NEED SOMEONE TO LEAN ON

We, humans, are herd animals. We need each other to survive and get by in a tough world like our own. Everyone needs to have a support system, people they can count on when life gets tough. Having a strong support system has many benefits such as better well-being, healthier coping skills, and a longer, healthier life.

If you are suffering from BPD, only you fully know how hard it is to live as yourself. No one understands borderline behavior unless they have lived with it. Questioning your abilities, your worth, and your identity every day, not knowing when your feelings will change at any given time or how you are going to feel in a while, being deeply afraid of abandonment, and worrying that the people whom you love and care about don't feel the same way for you. It makes thinking clearly and communicating rationally very difficult.

In its extremes, the people in your life won't understand how to help you, no matter how much they care about you. It's okay. You have what it takes to get better. As with all mental illnesses, to get better, you will require compassion and acceptance from yourself, family, friends, and strangers.

Similarly, a friend or family member of someone with BPD will often find themselves at a loss when it comes to helping them. They might feel helpless in merely trying to help at all. Their concern and efforts to intervene might offend them or come across as betrayal. It is nobody's fault in this situation.

The nature of BPD is such that it makes relationships stressful for everyone involved.

Family and friends of a person with BPD will often have questions as to how they can help their loved one. For this, social support systems are crucial to have. There are resources available to provide support groups with discussion forums, advice, emotional support, and assistance to family members, friends, caretakers, and loved ones of those with BPD. These resources are there to assist their understanding so they can better support and advocate for their loved ones living with BPD, and this would be in the best interest of everyone involved.

The benefits of having emotional support go both ways - for the provider as well as the one in need. The one who is providing it will need to be well-equipped and emotionally charged to look after the one in need, spend time with them, listen to and validate them, and offer practical help, sincere reassurance, and compassion.

# 3

# BORDERLINE PERSONALITY DISORDER - "WHAT DOES IT LOOK LIKE?"

## Deep dive into BPD traits and the subtypes

Borderline Personality Disorder is diagnosed using the DSM-5 manual - the *Diagnostic and Statistical Manual of Mental Disorders* states the nine criteria of the disease

### Frantic efforts to avoid real or imagined abandonment

"I was late to meet you for lunch and now you're upset with me. I have a feeling you're going to break up with me soon, aren't you? You hate me so you're going to leave me."

That is a prime example of anticipated or imagined abandonment. The Borderline jumps to the worst possible conclusion, expecting the very thing they fear the most to happen and it terrifies them. This can cause such immense anxiety that the way they start responding to their fear makes the thing they are so scared of happening, happen in real life. Their fear of the other person leaving makes them assume the worst and say out loud the bad things that they think will happen. Someone can only reassure them but that does not make the fear go away. This will frustrate the other person to the point where they might *want* to leave. Any type of disagreement from them over the Borderline's conclusions feels like proof to them that what they imagined is truly happening. It becomes a *self-fulfilling prophecy* - a phenomenon of someone "predicting" or expecting something to happen, such that the way they start behaving makes the thing actually happen.

A fear of abandonment is very human. No one likes being left alone. In BPD, the trait isn't merely fear. It is "frantic efforts to avoid real or imagined abandonment".

If such a fear of abandonment causes them to make such hasty and, rather, socially unacceptable choices in the way they address it or cope with the thought of it, then there is cause for concern.

For a person with BPD, the pain of loneliness can feel like such an unbearable, stinging ache that can only be relieved by the presence of a lover that promises never to let go.

Here's another scenario for an example. Their family says, "We need to shift some of your old stuff out of the house because there isn't much living space anymore. You'll be okay with that, right?"

To be more agreeable, they say yes but inside a panic arises. They start to think they are getting kicked out and think they cannot live there anymore, that they are a burden to them and they're better off homeless. They are scared of being ,but expect to be ,abandoned by their family.

This can shake the bonds the person with BPD has with their loved ones. If their loved ones were to ask them about how they feel and act because of their fears, they might admit that they do notice the pattern and how it negatively affects the relationship.

It is important to recognize TRIGGERS as logic and reasoning can very easily slip away when fear kicks in, which is why it's best to be prepared. It is a survival mechanism for the borderline person but it can have damaging outcomes.

**Unstable and intense interpersonal relationships, with marked shifts in attitudes toward others (from idealization to devaluation or from clinging dependency to isolation and avoidance), and prominent patterns of manipulation of others.**

This trait applies to all relationships - family and relatives, friendships, intimate relationships, and even the workplace. The borderline can start on a pleasing note - idealizing the person, wanting to be around them all the time, being dependent on them, being passionate and loving at first, clingy, etc. This sickly sweet shower of love and affection is not well-received by all. If the friend or partner wishes to have some space to themselves or if they get frustrated and pull away, the person with BPD can quickly switch to holding a lot of resentment or dislike for the friend or partner, passive treatment such as avoidance, and fear of intimacy.

People with BPD tend to think very little of themselves. They can put themselves down and express those feelings out loud. They can speak their mind by saying things such as: "I don't deserve to be loved or cared for". They can even doubt the care and compassion of a good friend, family member, or loving partner. This truly gets in the way of the bond Borderlines have with other people and makes it difficult for them to get close. As a matter of fact, it can cause them to pull away, especially if they are not aware of the complexity of BPD.

The BPD sufferer is torn between the longing for love to fill the gap of loneliness and their fear of losing themselves in letting someone else into their life. They are afraid they might lose themself, however much identity they do believe they have, their confidence and independence. On the other hand, they search constantly for "The One", the perfect lover who will give them their undivided time and attention, who they expect to be there for them all the time.

This can result in unsteady relationships as the borderline turns to manipulative tendencies to cope. Such as gaslighting (a type of manipulation where the manipulator causes the other person to question their own memory of an incident with them, their feelings, and perception), setting high and unrealistic expectations of others, excessive complaining, seeking sympathy, acting helpless or weak to get rescued.

Even threatening to hurt oneself or make suicidal gestures to gain attention.

One of the reasons why a person with BPD has difficulty in relationships is because they may lack the ability to learn from their past mistakes and may not be self-aware or observant of their own thought and behavior patterns. As a result, the same damaging patterns, which cause destructive relationships, are repeated.

## Marked and persistent identity disturbance manifested by an unstable self-image or sense of self.

Borderline Personality Disorder creates a lack of identity in the sufferer. It can dramatically waver the person's sense of self, causing *identity disturbance* or *disturbed personal identity* - a term used to define a person's disconnected and uncertain idea of self, of what "me", "I" or "myself" mean to them. It's like when they look in a mirror, they cannot see their reflection.

Identity disturbance presents itself in multiple ways. If you are suffering from BPD or experiencing this onset of symptoms, you would know all too well the struggle of finding yourself. Truthfully, you feel like you cannot find yourself. You feel like you are not anywhere to find as far as you're concerned. You do not know your place in this world. That is why you might be constantly searching for ways that do give you control over yourself such as changing your appearance, getting new haircuts, changing hair colors, shifting up your wardrobe, and even claiming a different name to be called by.

Identity disturbance can make a person with BPD go so far as to create different personas in their head so that they can pick and choose who they want to be as they please. A different person, a different mask. They can change their looks, their likes and dislikes, their name, and anything that makes up their personality. All that other people can see is someone who cannot make up their mind or someone who is making a fool out of themselves. However, the reality is that their idea of themselves is chaotic and incoherent. They are constantly trying to fill that void of confusion with desperate attempts to make themselves out to be *someone*. Some Borderlines will trade love and safety for the comfort of having an identity, and safekeeping it.

There is a constant battle against being "a fake" to achieve complete authenticity. "Fake it 'til you make it" is a common phrase many people follow to achieve confidence in their sense of self and their abilities. For example, a freshman in High school keeps his head up, smiles, and engages in introductions and small talk at his new school. Secretly, he struggles with social anxiety and is terrified if others were to see that aspect of him. His confidence grows as he starts to make friends and does not feel like he has to put up a front for others to like him anymore.

The person with BPD does not sit comfortably with the sense of "faking it" and is unable to gain confidence that way, even when they do gain liking from others. They are hyper-aware that they might be disingenuous and fear that others will notice it. It can almost feel fraudulent like they're being "wrong".

Sometimes, they change themselves to be liked by others. A different mask and personality for a different person. If someone is unhappy with them, there can be a feeling of self-hatred or anger that arises in the Borderline's mind. They rack their brain for what might be wrong with them while thinking, "I changed myself and acted just to fit your needs. I tried to be someone you would like!". They spiral while trying to figure out how they could have been "better" just to be easier and more digestible for the other person.

It takes a lot of effort to find an image of themselves they are happy with. They will work on it till they can deem it "perfect" and accept this as their identity. They will go to lengths to avoid circumstances that can change or soil that part of them - their self-image. Similarly, they go through as many options as they can in hopes of finding their place while searching for some comfort or satisfaction. They will change jobs, friends, their own name, or even experiment with their sexual preferences - sexual identity can also be confusing for the majority of borderline personalities. All in all, BPD sufferers can travel to extremes just to feel a sense of acceptance from others as well as themselves.

**Impulsiveness in at least two areas that are potentially self-destructive, e.g., substance abuse, sexual promiscuity, gambling, reckless driving, shoplifting, excessive spending, or overeating.**

Impulsivity in BPD refers to rapid and unplanned action. It means to seek pleasure with little or no regard for consequences. As a way of coping with emotional stress, people with BPD crave immediate gratification to escape and feel good or relieved, even if it can put a lot about their life at stake.

It is typically expressed, in individuals suffering from BPD symptoms ,in the forms of substance abuse, spending sprees, inappropriate outbursts of anger, unprotected or risky sex, self-harm such as cutting or burning, etc. There is even "quiet borderline behavior" that isn't the "usual" reckless impulsive behavior - not all people with BPD are comfortable with exaggerated outward expressions. This can be moving from one flat or house to another, changing careers or jobs, investing in hobbies at their financial expense, oversharing in real life or especially online while behind a screen, for example.

Another Borderline might also immerse themselves in short-lived obsessions such as dieting excessively, weight-watching, and caring for others too much at the cost of your own time and well being.

People with BPD are not able to account for consequences because, in the heat of a moment, they have very little regard for what the future holds and what mistakes they have made in the past. Their strong urge to act immediately is all they know at that time.

Borderlines are not able to connect the dots or realize patterns of repeated incidents in the past. They cannot calculate how their recklessness will backfire or cost them. They tend to repeat the same mistakes and when faced with the consequences, the guilt can eventually catch up.

## Recurrent suicidal threats, gestures, behavior, or self-mutilating behaviors

Self-harm and suicidal tendencies can indicate extreme depression in BPD:- the need to end their suffering. Suicidal threats or gestures are also features of BPD that are typically carried out as desperate attempts to gain the sympathy of others.

104 adolescent inpatients and 290 adult inpatients with BPD were interviewed. Among them, it was reported that the rate of self-mutilation was about 90% and the rate of suicide attempts was 75%. (Goodman, 2017)

As discussed previously, self-mutilation or self-harm is an impulsive action. Feelings of guilt or low self-worth can cause someone with BPD to self-inflict pain as a way of punishing themselves. Self-mutilation or self-harm is paradoxically a means of avoiding pain and sadness. The pain *temporarily* distracts them from their negative feelings. In other cases, self-inflicted pain can also be the only way they know how to feel again. It can be a means of escaping numbness when they lose touch with the sense of reality, which can be due to traumatic experiences or another feature of mental illness such as depression. The pain is what makes them feel real and grounded with reality. It reminds them that they exist and have control. Frequently, the pain sensation isn't strong enough to have that effect on them. In this case, frustration builds and they turn to more extreme attempts to self-induce a greater pain stimulus.

Many people with BPD admit they feel calm and relieved from their tension and anxiety after hurting themselves.

Self-inflicted pain can also function as a tool to ward off or distract Borderlines from unwanted feelings like loneliness. You might cut yourself on the limbs, abdomen, or chest to keep you from unwanted tendencies or thoughts and hope that the memory of pain would prevent this in the future as well. This can become habit-forming, and seeking relief in such a way can even become addictive.

For some, it can be a means of redemption. For instance, Sarah, who has disordered eating habits, felt guilty after she binged again and exceeded her set caloric intake for the day. She was afraid of gaining weight and felt sad that she couldn't restrict herself from eating all that food so she purged, making herself puke until all she could see coming out were blood and saliva. Sarah felt relieved and in control of herself only after getting all food out of her system, despite having gone through a lot of discomfort and pain.

Self-destructive behavior can also develop as a manipulative tendency to gain attention or sympathy in times of need. A para-suicidal attempt is a harmful act or attempt to self-harm that is meant to make it seem like someone wants to die, which is not meant to succeed. For instance, during a progressively escalating argument, a woman put a kitchen knife to her wrist and threatened to cut herself so her husband would drop the confrontation and apologize first.

## Affective instability due to marked reactivity of mood with severe episodic shifts to depression, irritability, or anxiety, usually lasting a few hours and only rarely more than a few days

Just what does this mean?

People with BPD, to an extreme degree, have an unstable emotional state. They can go from cheerful to sad to enraged all in the span of an hour. The difference is that neurotypicals ('normal' people) have a sound, steady way of thinking through things. For example, neurotypical people can also worry or feel sad about someone, whom they love, walking out of their life. They can feel sad about it for a few days, and cry it out but do they get angry at others because of it? Do they lose trust in everyone they know and everyone they will meet afterward? Do they feel like they're on the brink of death? No, not at all. But a person suffering from BPD has to go through that extreme wave of disturbance every time they do go through that kind of loss, even if they just imagine it. Their view of the world has a different shade, one that is more saturated and intense. Metaphorically, it is as though the same colors that everyone sees are much brighter, dizzying, and overwhelming for them, such that it causes them to react so strongly.

Tiny isolated details of an incident or event that remind the person with BPD of their unpleasant upbringing or a traumatic event, a negative comment or conversation can act as TRIGGERS, causing them to react or respond in a rash way that manifests as dysfunctional behavior e.g. silent treatment, blaming others, crying uncontrollably or lashing out.

## Chronic feelings of emptiness

"What's the point when we're all going to die, anyway?"

This kind of thought lives in the mind of a Borderline, especially in depressive moods.

They feel extreme boredom that cannot be satisfied by anything. The person with BPD struggling with this symptom does not see any point in doing anything, even if it used to bring them joy. For a black hole of apathy in the chest that seems to suck all hope and will to live, "empty" is an accurate word for describing the feeling.

It is as though they are at a gas station in need of fuel for their car. As soon as they fill the tank and get in the car, it doesn't start because the fuel evaporates right after they've filled it. It's a fuel tank that never fills and they're stuck at the gas station.

They feel they don't have what everyone else has which makes them human beings.

In frustration, the Borderline can let their impulsivity take the wheel and search for the one thing to fill the gaping hole inside and feel okay again. They'll try serial dating, turn to alcohol and drugs, and even self-mutilate to feel in touch with the sense of reality again, and that makes them more susceptible to suicidal attempts at the time. It is highly likely they will turn to risky behavior or dangerous situations to self-induce emotions like fear, sadness, and anger so they can feel alive again.

It is a feeling that can return and gnaw at the mind even after having a fun night out and dancing with friends. The minute they step inside their home and shut the door behind them, there's the empty feeling again. The enjoyment that would have left anyone else lasting satisfaction dissipates.

**Inappropriate, intense anger, or lack of control of anger, e.g., frequent displays of temper, constant anger, and recurrent physical fights.**

Inappropriate fits of rage or anger may be one of the most troubling symptoms of BPD. People with BPD experience a brighter shade of more intense anger than other people would. They are usually unpredictable and confusing for others. What triggers them would seem trivial and harmless to any observer and the borderline's destructive expression of anger does not seem to match up to what frustrates them.

Beneath it all lies the fears of abandonment, rejection, and disappointment. What's concerning is that this rage is often directed at precious close ones like family members or spouses, to their FP ,their "Favourite Person". This can repel the people that make up their support system, and which they are in dire need of. It can leave those people disturbed and questioning their safety. It takes strength for them to meet the challenge of choosing to stay and empathize but this is precisely what the Borderline craves.

It may be a defense mechanism that is activated as a response to being triggered by a situation that reminds them of their past trauma. It is known that BPD is significantly linked to childhood trauma and abuse for a lot of sufferers.

Besides family members, the borderline's anger and frustration can also be projected on their mental health care providers, making the treatment of BPD much more difficult than it already is.

## Transient, stress-related paranoid thoughts or symptoms of severe dissociation.

The psychotic state is one in which the person's thoughts and emotions are impaired to an extent where they lose touch with reality.

People with BPD commonly suffer from dissociation and *paranoid ideation* - a symptom that involves brief, stress-related paranoia characterized by experiences of feeling threatened or plotted against and suspicion.

Dissociation is a mental process where someone disconnects from their identity, their thoughts, and feelings, memories, or any of their five senses. Dissociation can be closely linked with a Borderline's other symptoms such as identity disturbance, impaired emotional regulation, and disturbed interpersonal relationships. It mainly happens when the mind is overwhelmed e.g., a person with BPD recalling their trauma during therapy. It can even occur during stressful situations or surroundings. The brain has a built-in function where it blocks out memories of pain.

What sets psychosis in BPD apart from psychosis in other mental illnesses such as schizophrenia or manic depression is that it is briefer in borderlines and their break from reality can dissolve in a matter of minutes or hours, after which they return to their senses.

## THE 4 TYPES OF BORDERLINE PERSONALITY DISORDER

BPD in its pure form is a mental health disorder of emotional and interpersonal relationship dysfunction. Types of BPD can appear similar in presentation, with variability in some symptoms such as intense displays of anger, impulsivity and aggressiveness.

There are four accepted types of Borderline Personality Disorder: discouraged, self-destructive, impulsive, and petulant.

## Discouraged/Quiet BPD

People with this type struggle with a remarkably intense fear of abandonment. They tend to keep their emotions inside rather than displaying them, and are likely to self-blame rather than point fingers at others. They may also take extreme measures to avoid or prevent abandonment.

Discouraged or quiet types can often feel like they don't belong or that they don't have any sustainable bonds with others. As much as they wish to feel accepted and loved, it's difficult because they are prone to self-isolate. They may often feel lonely and a sense of emptiness that lingers, and that distances them more from others. Due to insecurity and low self-worth, signs and symptoms of depression are going to be present.

Discouraged types many struggle with constant feelings of weakness and helplessness, which aligns with symptoms of their depression as well. They can end up showing excessive dependence on others, which shows up as clinginess or neediness. In the case that their fear of abandonment and rejection are triggered, emotional mood swings and anger may come forward.

## Self-destructive BPD

People engage in self-destructive behaviors as a result of feelings of worthlessness, childhood trauma or a lack of secure attachments.

People with self-destructive BPD struggle with low self-esteem, extreme self-hatred and appear bitter. They are prone to self-harming and suicidal behavior.

When they engage in reckless and impulsive behaviors, it is out of a lack of care for themselves and not to impress others. They can be overcome with an increase in energy and a reduced need for sleep. They lack the sense of care for themselves so they sabotage their own wellbeing and happiness. Due to their extremely low self-esteem, they feel like they don't deserve good things. They are also of the belief that no one else cares about them, and so they don't have to care about themselves either. Further examples of self-destructive BPD type behaviors include: threatening suicide, self-harm, substance abuse and risky, dangerous activities.

## Impulsive BPD

Impulsivity in this type means quick and unplanned action along with little regard for the outcome or consequences. Impulsive types can appear charismatic, charming and captivating, like a magnetic force. They come off as superficial and entertain others with ease. One thing that they do like is motivating others and engaging with them. They enjoy being at the center of attention and seeking out thrill.

Unfortunately, they're prone to take part in risky, dangerous behaviors without thought of the future, such as binging food or overspending, reckless driving, drinking and substance use, gambling, lashing out, throwing fits of anger, and fighting.

## Petulant BPD

Petulant types have difficulty expressing feelings. There is a high mark of emotion dysregulation, and petulant types struggle with intense mood swings and outbursts of anger. They can quickly go from being angry at one moment to feeling gloomy the next.

Relationships are not easy for the petulant types. They tend to feel that they don't deserve love and affection. Another occurrence is the unhealthy desire to steer the relationship and control where it's going, which is accompanied by a dissatisfaction in relationships as well. The fear of abandonment can be so extreme that the petulant type may pose ultimatums in the relationship, or test their partner for proof whether or not they still love them. It's like a constant push and pull motion in the relationship from their side. The petulant borderline may also show characteristics of *covert narcissism* - subtle narcissism in which someone craves admiration and lacks empathy for others.

# 4

# CAUSES OF BPD - "WHY AM I LIKE THIS?"

## It's not your fault

"Did something happen to me or was I born like this?"
"What makes my brain and personality the way that it is?"

If you're starting to question yourself, it means you're willing to work on yourself and gain more awareness, which is practically half the work being done toward betterment, so you're on the right track. You might wonder why you behave in ways that don't make any sense to you, why you do or say bizarre things, which do not align with your morals and values. It frustrates you when people that are trying to help you ask, "what's wrong?" because you aren't so sure what's wrong yourself. You just know that you're not quite right and you aren't able to put a finger on why exactly you are the way you are, even when you wish you could change.

Listen, it makes sense. It isn't your fault that your brain is the way that it is.

Having an explanation for your behaviors will likely help you live an easier life with BPD - a chronic, persistent and maladaptive dysregulation of emotions and interpersonal relationships. You will be able to connect the dots to form a clearer, bigger picture of just who you are.

Let's start by agreeing that mental illness is profoundly stigmatized. As discussed, there is no ultimate diagnostic tool or litmus test that can concretely diagnose BPD or any other mental illness as a matter of fact. Considering that mental illness is not exactly 'visible' since its symptoms don't present physically the way they would for a handicapped person who needs to use crutches to walk or the debilitating state of a cancer patient undergoing chemotherapy, it's very difficult to evidence or prove that you have BPD.

However, we can still give credit to fMRI scans - which stands for functional Magnetic Resonance Imaging Scan, and which is a way doctors and psychologists can scan a brain and see what different parts of it activate more than others when the person being scanned is engaged by a task that prompts them to think or feel. For instance, in people with BPD, studies have shown that parts of the brain that regulate emotions and store memory are almost 16% smaller than normal, particularly suggesting that experiences of trauma can lead to such changes. (Lis et al., 2007) fMRI scans cannot diagnose mental disorders on their own but they do verify that there is a biological factor that plays a role in the cause of mental illness, that the person afflicted with a mental disorder is not 'making it up', that your diagnosis is *valid* and it's backed up by science.

No one gets to choose and pick what disease they get in life. The disease activates with no warning whatsoever. BPD is a pathology of the mind with real causes just like the rest of the many diseases that can occur in the body. Mental illness does not discriminate. Your symptoms can flare up and burn holes in the fabric of your everyday life. But your disease is not a failing on your part, it's a struggle you're afflicted with and you have in your hands the choice to seek help and take responsibility. You *will* get better.

Essentially, there is no fault in your person-hood or even your personality. This is not a personality flaw. BPD is somewhat misleading in the way people use it as a label which implies that it's a flaw in the sufferer's personality. This means people with BPD may gain a negative perception of themselves and have to deal with the silent pain of internalized stigma in addition to the emotional suffering brought on by their disease. Even healthcare providers and clinicians can be reluctant to treat people with BPD due to the stigma that society has plugged with it. Some clinicians will even reject treating those suffering from BPD because they view them as unwilling to help themselves, unpredictable, and even manipulative, although it's not like they're deliberately manipulative.

Stigma makes it extremely difficult for people with BPD to have a fair chance of seeking help. No wonder they would act defensively on being approached regarding their disorder. They don't have the capacity to deal with judgement from others.

There is a neuro-biological basis for this disorder that can explain the majority of the functional abnormalities accompanying BPD. There is a structure to this disorder that you can familiarize with, understand and educate yourself on. You will learn that you, as a person, are not your disease. Educating yourself on the facts and science of BPD will help you seek help and cope with the difficulties it brings along with it. BPD is a disease in the brain that can be treated. You, as a person, are not broken. While the causes of this disorder are beyond your control, there is still hope to have in the fact that there is help. You can overcome the struggles and difficulties of living with BPD with the right help. This emotional suffering will not last forever. You have it in you to get better. Research unfolds several major factors to be causes of BPD, including environmental and social factors i.e. deficient parenting, childhood neglect, trauma and abuse, and biological vulnerability involving genetics.

## UPBRINGING AND CHILDHOOD TRAUMA

The early environment every person grows up in strongly contributes to their conditioning and beliefs. A child that has been deprived of love, care, and validation while growing up will likely have low self-esteem and tend to feel alienated. Growing up neglected, not having your feelings validated, and feeling unimportant will have lasting effects on your ability to trust, which gives rise to the fear that others will inevitably hurt and disappoint you. Not having received enough love and affection can also impact the person's ability to love and care for others.

The type of early environment, usually that of a family, that contributes most to BPD is known as, "the invalidating environment." The people in an invalidating environment are typically hostile, emotionally neglecting, abusive, and overly critical on a long-term basis.

Object constancy refers to the attitudes we have toward interpersonal relationships. It is the ability to believe that a relationship can be stable and functional despite occasional conflict, distance, or disagreements.

Growing up with inconsistent and non-empathic parents, pre-borderline children may fail to develop a stable view of themselves or others that they can look at to reassure themselves or understand that just because something isn't working out does not mean it is hopeless. People with BPD have poor object constancy, and that can explain why they have an intense fear of abandonment and unstable interpersonal relationships. One of the reasons why this is the case can be traced back to their upbringing.

Abuse is one of the strongest causes of trauma and a hallmark of childhood neglect. It is a tragic situation that undoubtedly affects a child's emotional development.

Growing up in a household around abusive caregivers or other family members, you never know what might trigger an outburst of anger or earn you a punishment.

You feel that your emotions are invalid or that you deserve unfair treatment. Being a victim of emotional, physical, or sexual abuse as a child leaves you feeling unsafe and confused. The fear that is instilled from being subject to abuse activates a fight-or-flight response, and if the abuse is chronic then that response doesn't turn off and fractures the person from trauma. When you were young, did your mother help you up after you'd trip and wipe your tears, or did she yell at you to stop crying? Did your father help you with homework and reassure you after you'd fail a test, or did he scold you for not doing as well as the rest of your classmates? These are examples of negative incidents that can affect the view you have of yourself.

Growing up around abuse, especially from parents or care-givers, may have instilled in you feelings of inadequacy, in spite of best efforts to please others, a lack of emotional boundaries, feeling responsible for your parents' happiness, feeling guilty for your own happiness, anxiety and hyper-vigilance due to abusive household or circumstances being unpredictable.

However, it is worth noting that not everyone with BPD is subject to abuse in their childhood and not everyone that has been abused goes on to develop BPD.

Stressful or traumatic life events at a young age lead to the conditioning of beliefs about yourself and other people that can become harmful and the cause for distress. For instance, you felt that you deserved to be punished or physically abused if you were caught in trouble ,because you've grown accustomed to that treatment from your parents when facing consequences. Traumatic experiences may include often feeling invalidated, unsupported, or afraid, being caught in the middle of family difficulties or having parents with substance abuse problems, or any form of abuse such as sexual, physical, emotional, or verbal.

Not everyone who experiences trauma or abuse will develop a mental disorder. However, trauma is a common and crucial risk factor that plays a role in the development of the disease. In some, it can act as a trigger that activates the mental illness that the person might already be genetically predisposed to.

Some people with BPD haven't experienced particularly distressing treatment or abuse from their caregivers while growing up. But childhood neglect can also be a contributing factor.

Childhood emotional neglect is defined as, "a childhood characterized by the lack of or an absence of enough emotional validation, emotional attention and emotional responsiveness from one's parent." One or more parents are gone for an extended period, divorce, the child is left alone to take care of themselves, etc. Children have emotional needs while growing up, especially children that are more sensitive than others. When parenting is deficient or the child's emotional needs are not catered to sufficiently, it can create a strong sense of invalidation in the child such as not being seen or heard. Neglect can also be *perceived* such as when the child might not get praised or encouraged very much for doing well in school, or when they don't get treated to snacks. In this case, the person hasn't failed to provide the child with their basic needs but the child's perception still influences them nonetheless.

Although childhood neglect is not an officially listed contributing factor to BPD itself, it does contribute to social or environmental factors that might have predisposed the person to BPD.

Emotionally neglected children typically grow up in a household that isn't very receptive to emotions. When they aren't noticed or responded to enough, they might take it that their feelings don't matter. So, to cope, they push their feelings down or bottle them up to avoid feeling like a burden. These children can grow up to be out of tune with their feelings and grow up to struggle with emotions as adults, not knowing how to express or cope with them. This can lead to feelings of emptiness and a lack of emotional skills.

A child looks up to their primary caregivers while growing up at home. They are observant of the way their parents and family members interact, what emotions they express and to what extent, how they respond to those emotions, and how they react in different situations.

A household where negative feelings are suppressed and kept bottled up rather than being talked about can hold a lot of tension. Family members can be reluctant to voice their concerns, fearing that they'll be judged, that they might make others unhappy, or even worse, get ignored. When a child sees this and grows used to it, they won't have an example of healthy emotional behavior or stable relationships to refer to. They might grow up to feel lost in dealing with such aspects of life themselves.

Those that develop BPD are often raised in a household with extreme childhood neglect. In some cases, not only is the child dismissed or invalidated but they are also punished for having normal feelings. In some cases where parents were absent or unavailable, perhaps working overtime, struggling with alcohol and drug abuse, or a mental illness, the child would have to look after themselves, other family members such as younger siblings, and even their parents. Having to learn to be responsible from a young age and learning to take care of others means being neglected.

The primary outcome of emotional neglect is that children might not grow up learning about emotions; or how to identify, manage, use, or express them in healthy ways. Unhealthy emotional development may cause the person to reject their feelings, leading to a weak sense of self.

No one is perfect. All parents are new at one point and may not get everything right the first time. Parents can have their shortcomings too such as being too strict or not being strict enough, not being fully attentive, being forgetful, or losing their patience with their child. However, when some lines are crossed over to downright hostile, abusive, and targeting behaviors, that is where the problems arise. Deficient parenting creates a difficult family environment and it can cause stunted emotional development for the child in it.

The trauma a child or young person suffers may ,of course,be more obvious in the form of physical,sexual or emotional abuse. This is not necessarily at the hands of their caregiver. They may have been abused by,for example, another family member,a teacher or a stranger. The trauma doesn't have to take the form of abuse.It could be an event which has an immense emotional impact such as a death or being the victim of a disaster. If the trauma remains untreated, and therefore unresolved ,this may begin to manifest in the development of the traits of BPD in adolescence. Even if the traits are evident ,there remains a reluctance ,amongst many mental health professionals,to diagnose during the teens and so the traits may be untreated ,worsening over time.

## ON THE SCIENCE BEHIND BPD: ROLES OF BIOLOGY AND GENETICS

### Genetics: what are genes and how do they cause BPD?

What do genes have to do with the development of BPD?

A gene is the small part from the code of life present in all the cells of your body that help determine a trait you might have, like the color of your eyes. Genes make you up as a whole person.

You inherit your genes directly from your parents, who inherit their genes from their parents, pass those down to you, and so on. In this way, you can inherit the gene for a disease someone in your immediate family had. So if someone in your family has mental health issues this increases the chances of you developing the same disease at some point in your life.

Research shows that those of us that have a family member with BPD, particularly first-degree such as a parent or sibling, are 10 times more likely to have it ourselves. Although we can't be too sure if the cause is purely genetic if that is the case, especially if that family member resides in the same environment as we have grown up in. In that case, the cause can even be environmental or related to upbringing. There are no absolutes. It's hard to tell if the problems associated with BPD are inherited or caused by the environment or your cognition, as in the ways that you think, behave or cope with life, having learned those ways from people around you. So first-degree relatives not only share genes, but environments as well ,such as how siblings are raised by the same parents.

The fact that someone else in the family has BPD does point to the genetic predisposition of it, but it does not mean that the cause of BPD can be pinned on the genetic factor alone. In most cases, it is the interaction of genes and environment that lead to the development of BPD in people with the disorder.

Evidence suggests that there are changes brought on by experiences of childhood trauma that can occur in genes. This implies that one's upbringing and environmental factors can have an impact on genes.

## The biology of your brain

Someone with BPD who is emotionally vulnerable can have a high physical sensitivity to emotions as well. The person's sympathetic nervous system, the system in the brain that prepares your body for fight-or-flight, is triggered easily by regular emotions. The reaction can be very intense, skyrocketing the person's breathing and heart rate, they start to sweat and the feeling of impending doom starts to take over. This can explain why people with BPD experience mood swings and panic attacks or frequent bouts of anxiety.

Another biological predisposition to BPD can be illustrated by difficulty regulating emotions. This can mean having difficulty controlling impulses and prioritizing long-term reward over short-term gratification, finding it hard to stop oneself from acting immediately in response to strong emotions, resisting self-destructive behavior in coping with strong emotions, and so much more.

Borderlines are susceptible to emotion dysregulation in that the strategies they are likely to use to cope with strong emotions are not the helpful kind. These strategies include rumination which is to focus or hyper-fixate on emotions, suppression and avoidance of strong emotions. Higher rumination is likely to increase the chances of the person with BPD engaging in harmful behaviors, such as self-harm or substance abuse, as a means of coping. It goes to say that the 'feeling parts' of the brain in someone with BPD are hyper-sensitive to emotional experiences.

There is a lot of research underway to get to the bottom of the biological basis of BPD. Whether it's neurotransmitters, brain functions, genetic or other predisposing health conditions, something biologically about the person with this disorder is causing them to have a greater sensitivity to emotions and life changes. This sensitivity is what can lead them to have a life-long struggle with strong reactions, difficulty in sustaining relationships and other aspects of their life, and intense mood changes.

Parts of the brain responsible for emotion regulation, impulsivity, and aggression in people with BPD are different from those in neurotypicals. There is less activation in parts of the brain that are associated with the control of emotions, but greater activation in parts of the brain responsible for reactivity, types of emotional response and other brain functions.

Say you're driving when a car cuts you in the middle of the road and speeds away. You feel a spark and surge of rage coming on. "That bastard! How could he?!"

Or you feel insulted by an unsolicited comment someone made on your appearance.

The emotional response in instances such as these can be explained by the "amygdala" which is a little almond-shaped structure, one on each side of the brain.

In addition, these reactions are essentially brought about by parts of the brain called, "the limbic system.", which includes the amygdala among other structures. The limbic system serves the purpose of acting as the main control center that specializes in emotional matters. It directs the ways we feel and think. The limbic system also includes the hippocampus, which is responsible for learning, memory, and stress regulation.

Before we continue here, let me reassure you that there is no need to be intimidated by these new words or this sciencey information. Think of this as a discussion of how the parts of a unique machine work differently than they would in most machines. Similarly, there are differences in the structure and activation of some of the feeling and thinking parts of the brain between those with a mental illness such as BPD and those without.

The amygdala reads and produces the emotional aspects of situations. Tears, an emotional signal that indicates sadness, anger, or immense joy, are triggered by the amygdala. When you go about anything in life, your mental processes are constantly being engaged. In picking up on senses and stimulation from the surrounding environment or the people in it, the amygdala asks "Do I like this? Is this something that can hurt me? Am I afraid of this thing?"

If your feelings point to a "yes" in any way, the amygdala is an alarm system that trips and alerts other parts of your brain to make you act out or retreat i.e. the fight-or-flight response. The amygdala's ability to trigger an emotional emergency can cause it to trip the rational mind as well as control the body's natural functions such as breathing, heart rate and sweating.

Additionally, there is also evidence that points to how the chemicals that are responsible for emotion regulation such as dopamine and serotonin do not work properly or have the same effects in the brain of someone with BPD.

## How does stress change the brain?

The part of the brain known as the "hippocampus" is mainly responsible for learning and memory processes i.e. recalling information, as well as the regulation of stress hormones.

Chronic stress affects the structure and function of the hippocampus. Over time, the stress of uncontrollable situations can interact with the hippocampus in a way such that the hippocampus shrinks and the production of stress regulation hormones is affected. So, as you can tell now, excessive and chronic stress can shake up the stress-regulating part of the brain and have significant effects, particularly in mental illnesses such as depression, generalized anxiety disorder and BPD.

BPD is found to be associated with high stress. The stress can be from the drastic mood changes, fears of abandonment and rejection, trouble in relationships, and all else you can find in the sea of suffering BPD can bring about.

Studies that looked into how prolonged stress across one's lifetime impacts the brain's, particularly the hippocampus, activation found that the more stress someone experiences, the lower the size of their hippocampus.

Keeping in view these points and the talk about what is causing BPD, it is safe to say that the dysregulation in mood results from a dysfunction in the brain, as well as from events in one's childhood.

# 5

# LIVING WITH BPD - WHAT IT LOOKS AND FEELS LIKE

## Behaviors and feelings: what to expect?

"Chaos" is a key word. Borderline Personality Disorder is a disorder of emotional and interpersonal dysregulation. In simple terms, it is an emotional and mental disease that lacks awareness and is generally difficult to diagnose. You cannot truly know what it is like to live with BPD unless you've lived with it yourself. It isn't possible to simplify BPD and present an "in a nutshell" version.

Mental illness cannot be shooed away. It sticks like flour dough you cannot wash off your hands and it can very well jam the gears of your mind as well as your life when left untreated. No problem has ever been solved by ignoring it. So let's talk about what matters here. What is it like for a person with BPD?

Something worth noting is that Borderlines cannot control when any emotion comes, how long it will stick around, and whether or not its effect will hurt or help them. This goes to say for the ones living with BPD as well as those looking out for someone they know with BPD: the fact is that you cannot control anyone else's emotions or reactions.

People with BPD feel emotions more easily and deeply. Sometimes when a Borderline is hurting, all they can do is just feel through it or let their waves of emotion crash over them because that's how intense it can be. It can be stressful for the sufferer's loved ones ,be that their FP or family or a partner,because all they wish to do is fix what's bothering them. However, sometimes there's nothing that can be done to help except for the loved ones to simply be there and experience the difficult time with them.

Some people with BPD who have lived through abuse and trauma try to fix their past. They feel guilty and overbearing for needing someone to take care of them or hoping to be loved because they never received enough of that growing up.

As a Borderline, you would know that feeling lonely or alone is unbearably miserable. Knowing you're being irrational is confusing and difficult to stop all by yourself. There is a loud, relentless inner child who is desperately asking to feel wanted and validated. This craving for validation can only be dealt with by being projected externally.

Part of BPD is the mirroring or copying of voices, styles, or behaviors of people, whether they're real or not, because you feel you never developed a personality of your own so you had to fashion one for yourself out of whatever you could gather. Still, no matter how hard you're trying or what you're doing, it will never feel right.

People living with BPD, who are able to manage the worst symptoms and regain stability through consistent efforts to seek help, still struggle with the idea of who they really are.

Sometimes you feel so content and happy, that you look forward to being okay again. Before you know it, something that isn't even necessarily bad happens and you feel your world falling apart. Your sky is clouded, your chest feels heavy and your mood has spiked, again. BPD comes with all-or-nothing thinking, that's also known as black-and-white thinking, where thoughts and feelings oscillate between extremes of either "Everything is great! Things are looking up!" or "Everything is terrible, and life is a disaster."

You wouldn't want to wish BPD on your worst enemy. It is not something anyone would want to have. Having BPD feels like a black hole that sucks up everything, even the light. It's an endless void that you can never fill.

## WHAT IT LOOKS LIKE ON THE OUTSIDE VERSUS WHAT IT ACTUALLY FEELS LIKE

Self-harm is a very taboo topic and not many people talk about it. People with BPD that do engage in self-harm will be reluctant to open up about it because of the fear of being labeled as "attention-seeking" when that is never the case. In reality, for some people, self-harm is rather a shout for help. For many, it is an impulse, and it just "feels like the right thing" to act on at the moment. The mind inflates the very idea of it until the person finally gives in to hurting themselves and feeling the pain. It is an unhealthy way of coping with emotional pain and intense anger that gives a momentary sense of satisfaction, relief, and escape from all the noise inside a person's head.

It might not be easy for someone to even be aware when a Borderline is harming themselves. Looking at a person's lifestyle can give away whether they are engaging in self-harm or if they are at risk of doing so in the future. The aspect that ties itself with self-harm belief systems are those such as having beliefs that are limiting, irrational, or not backed by any facts. These beliefs are ingrained in different people for different reasons but a common basis can be that of upbringing and childhood trauma. For instance, a person with BPD that grew up in an abusive household, or with parents that were unavailable due to being overworked, suffering from mental illness, or negligent behavior, may hold the belief that they don't deserve to feel loved by others.

As a Borderline, there are times when you might find yourself acting cold toward others, showing little care or interest in what others have to say. It isn't because you're trying to be mean or come off as rude. You aren't being deliberately impolite. You might simply be blank-faced or numb to yourself, others, and what's happening around you. This totally blank state can be a part of the mood switches or dissociation You may switch between moods such as being extremely happy, angry or sad, irritable, or just plain neutral even.

Speaking of which, mood switching is a constant struggle for people with BPD. Considering that one of the major functions that BPD disables in a person is emotion regulation, the person with BPD struggles to go about their day without their moods getting in the way. This means going between feeling on top of the world and looking forward to the day, suddenly being full of dread and wanting to go home, depressed, and then being completely fine for no particular reason at all. People that know you would be familiar with your mood switches and how you can be. However, to the people that don't know you, they will find it bizarre. Sometimes you won't be able to help these shifts, even when you want to and once they become apparent and attract attention from others, it will be difficult and awkward trying to explain, or even getting out of not explaining when you aren't comfortable with sharing. You can go from zero to level 100 in feeling anything whether it is love or spite, happy or sad, excitement or nervousness.

Another perception about people with BPD is that they are generally 'moody' or grumpy people, that they have a difficult temperament or they're unapproachable and not to be reckoned with. People that suffer from BPD are not like this,

BPD just *affects* their mood. The other term used to refer to this is, "emotionally unstable". You may be aware that BPD is sometimes known as Emotionally Unstable Personality disorder.

Borderlines can get easily upset at times, owing to their overall sensitivity and difficulty in regulating their emotions. How they respond to the situation is affected by how deeply they can feel. Many people find it difficult or don't have the capacity to understand and care for Borderlines .There can be a huge communication gap. They have a need for validation that may come from trauma, feelings of not being wanted . When those experiences are translated into adulthood, the person with BPD wants to be reassured that they are wanted or that they aren't being annoying by being around you, that they are not a bad person or a burden, and that they simply are cared for.They want to know they wont be abandoned. For someone with BPD, it is very easy to have the belief that people do not like them or that they are 'too much'. Typically struggling to maintain a consistent self-image that pleases themselves as well as others, their insecurities can get the best of them, however lovely they might be at other times.

It has been established so far that a lot of people suffering from BPD can be triggered by fears of being abandoned, betrayed, or cheated on. Stress-inducing triggers can activate unsound, self-critical beliefs. One of those beliefs is that they will be let down or let go of by people they care about. What can also be triggered is 'paranoid ideation', which is a symptom of BPD. Paranoid thoughts in someone with BPD can present, for example, as being afraid that a group of people near you are talking about you. The trigger can be anything such as a text from your friend reading, "we need to talk", the tone of someone's voice, a look from a stranger across the room that could've been mistaken for a glare, or when someone doesn't pick up your call.

Catastrophic thinking takes over which is where you think up irrational, worst-case outcomes. Being paranoid, you assume everyone is against you and you feel the need to be on high-alert and extra observant or watchful of other people's behavior or even the tone of their voice.

## RISK FACTORS FOR SELF-HARM AND SUICIDE

In any case, there is never a standalone, single risk factor that predisposes someone to suicidal thoughts or self-harm. Self-harm occurs when the emotions pile on so high, like a bucket that's filling to its brim and starting to overflow, that the person becomes desperate in looking for ways out of their emotional build-up, or to numb the pain. Self-harm and suicide are ways that people suffering from mental illness will take on as a way to escape their pain. The difference is that self-harm is when people deliberately hurt themselves, and suicide is the attempt to escape by dying.

Signs and symptoms of self-harm include:

- Scars
- Fresh cuts and scratches or burns
- Tugging at skin
- Always in possession of a sharp object, emotional instability, impulsivity, and behavioral unpredictability
- Statements of worthlessness or helplessness

Risk factors for self-harm and suicidal behavior in people with BPD include older age, suicide attempts in the past, antisocial personality traits or comorbidity, high impulsivity, greater susceptibility to depressive moods, and substance abuse disorders or alcoholism.

BPD sufferers with a history of self-harm or self-mutilating behavior had about twice the rate of suicide than those without. (Oumaya, 2008) Those that repeatedly self-harm increase their dependency in a positive feedback loop as the craving grows while the threshold for pain increases along with pain tolerance. Repetitive self-harm also starts making the sufferer start to feel as though it's the only escape from their emotional turmoil. So at any affliction or inconvenience, they experience dysphoria and like an itch they need to scratch, they turn to self-harm for relief. With time, they begin to underestimate the seriousness of their self-harming tendencies and behaviors to the point that they risk increasing the intensity as well as the frequency of their suicidal thoughts.

Feelings of depression, hopelessness, intense emotional insta-bility, and the general sense of a lack of control make sufferers of BPD more prone to suicidal thoughts and ideation.

Although not specifically in relation to people with BPD, those with antisocial traits or personality are relatively likely to attempt suicide because they are also likely to have a higher range of negative emotions and less self-control.

Substance abuse and self-harm are profoundly interlinked in that substance abuse leads to self-harm. Substances instil a feeling of relief or a "high" which causes people to lose self-control. Drugs worsen anxiety and depression, which makes matters worse since their exacerbation can contribute to more risky behaviors.

A lack of self-control is a contributing factor to self-harming tendencies. Especially since the harm inflicted by substance abuse is often calculated or even acknowledged by the person indulging.

When we visited the causes of BPD, we discussed that envi-ronmental factors, childhood trauma, and upbringing majorly contribute to the development of the disease. Well, these circumstances are also the risk factors that increase the chances of self-harming behavior in people with BPD.

One way is that BPD makes the person more impulsive and thus, prone to engaging in riskier or reckless behaviors. On the other hand, abuse or trauma can cause dissociation. Dissociation is when the person experiences separation or a disconnect from their senses, memories, thoughts, feelings, and reality. It affects the person's sense of identity and impulse control. Dissociation feels like you have taken the backseat in your own car while it is driving on its own. It is a way that the brain protects itself by allowing the person to escape inside their own head as a way of dealing with sudden or chronic, extreme stress or coping with trauma. Trauma is apparently the root cause of dissociation. A person with BPD who has been subject to abuse or trauma in their life may be prone to experiences of this state, especially when they have been triggered by real-life events or something that has reminded them of the same trauma ,their brain works to protect them from.

## STIGMA AND MISCONCEPTIONS

What does the term 'borderline' entail and how is it used to describe this type of personality disorder? In its origin, 'borderline personality' was referred to being on the border or the line between psychosis or neurosis. The word psychosis is used to describe conditions where the mind is affected in a way that the person can be delusional, paranoid or dissociated and there is a loss of touch with reality. On the other hand, neurosis refers to an inability to regulate emotions, and overall sadness. BPD is essentially a combination of parts from both psychosis as well as neurosis, in addition to other patterns of instability.

"Borderline personality disorder" as a name does not easily give away what the mental disorder is *really* about, and that can confuse people. This confusion adds to the stigma that is already deep-rooted and ever-growing in society.

People, that dismiss the struggles of someone living with a mental illness like BPD are not helpful in any way by saying things like, "Yeah, but so what? Everyone has problems. Some people have it worse like there are children that are starving!"

All that accomplishes is to make Borderlines feel guilty, more than they already do, for how they feel. It makes them feel like they were wrong to talk about their problems and open up in the first place, that they should be hiding their pain because someone else has it worse.

Yes, as a matter of fact, some people in this world are not very kind. Some people don't have the best intentions or they aren't conscious of the toxic behaviors that hurt those around them. However, a BPD diagnosis does not, even in the slightest bit, mean that the person with it has to be manipulative. Manipulative behavior and BPD are not synonymous.

Mental illness comes attached with stigmas that include misinformed beliefs, mainly due to a lack of awareness or willingness from others to learn more. People with BPD face stigma from many people such as beliefs that they are dangerous, immoral, incapable of taking care of themselves and others, aggressive, difficult to work with, that they do not want to get better, and are attention-seeking, or manipulative.

Unfortunately, they also face stigma from healthcare workers and mental health providers. This kind of stigma is harmful and downright unfair. It leads to a lack of hope in recovery, exacerbation of the negative and inaccurate perceptions of people with BPD, ineffective treatments, increases in treatment failures, and last but not least, worsening the health, as well as fears of abandonment ,for people with BPD.

Additionally, there is a confusion that arises between BPD and bipolar disorder. Bipolar disorder is a common misdiagnosis among people with BPD. Granted, there are similarities between the two such as mood swings, impulsivity, and increased risk for self-harm and suicide, but the main difference that sets BPD apart from bipolar disorder is the time duration of the mood shifts. People with bipolar disorder stay in their manic or depressive phases for weeks or months at a time, whereas the mood switches in BPD can occur within minutes or hours. The mood switches that can occur in a given time period are far more diverse e.g. anger, happiness, sadness, joy, frustration, etc in people with BPD.

## WHAT IS SPLITTING?

Splitting is a phenomenon where the person with BPD will either see things as "all good" or "all bad" without any gray area or in between. It happens abruptly, and the root cause is usually an external stimulus,a TRIGGER .

A person with BPD can 'split' themselves, where they see either the good or bad in them and never as a complex, whole being. When they split against their own selves, that can play into the unstable view of self.

This way of thinking is commonly applied to the people in a Borderline's life. Alternatively, when it comes to people, splitting can also be thought of in terms of 'demonization and idealization' instead of the 'black-and-white thinking' which is essentially the other side of the same coin in this topic of discussion.

Splitting may go a bit like this - your FP ,whom you considered to be the closest, most favorite and dearest to you, didn't get back to you on time or wasn't there for you when you expected them to be. You feel like they don't love you the same, that you have been betrayed and you're no longer safe with them. It is as though you were just flung from a place of total love and admiration for a person to turning downright spiteful or angry at them. This can all happen within a day,within an hour,even within minutes. That skip happened without giving the other person any benefit of the doubt, or stopping to think, "Perhaps I'm not the problem and they just got caught up in their own stuff."

Splitting can be a defense mechanism, particularly for those people with BPD that experienced trauma in their early life.

Every child is still in their developmental phase in all aspects that are psychological, mental, physical, and emotional. They are dependent on external influences to shape their mind and personality, and sources to fulfil their needs and desires. In the case of an abusive caregiver, the child sees two versions of the caregiver - a kind, safe version where they are not in a mood and aren't lashing out at the child, and a scary, dangerous version where they may be neglecting the child's needs or projecting their anger at them,even abusing them in some way. It is difficult for a young child to reconcile both those versions to create a perception of that person as a whole, to understand the dynamics of the person and their versions collectively to know how they work, to be able to think about their previous encounters with that person to relate to why they might be acting the way they are. That inability to relate and integrate different parts of a person is where their 'splitting' comes from. Therefore, that tendency to split can generalize and be carried forward.

DBT is known for effectively treating BPD, and one of the reasons is that this type of psychotherapy works to integrate different viewpoints and form a 'whole', to establish that the world is gray and that not everything is strictly on opposite ends, that there *is* a spectrum and a 'middle area'. To help someone with BPD who is going through a splitting episode and dwelling on their negative impression of the other person, it may be helpful to remind them of the reasons that made them like the person in the first place, or the qualities of the person that gained their admiration.

# FAVOURITE PEOPLE

It is perfectly human to be extra fond of someone that is giving you what you're looking for, and a neurotypical person is able to understand that the person they like will not always be catering to them, or be someone that they want them to be. The neurotypical can have a consistent and balanced view of another person. This is frequently very difficult for Borderlines especially in relation to their Favourite Person, their FP. Borderlines can become very dependent on their FP, put them on a pedestal, see only their good attributes. It is as if this relationship validates the FP: they are in a friendship with someone so great, and who thinks they're great too. The presence of the FP in the life of the Borderline helps fill the void of loneliness and isolation and is a distraction from feelings of self-doubt or self-loathing:-if such a wonderful person likes me, I must be kind of alright.

Consequently, when the FP doesn't live up to the Borderline's expectations or behaves in a way that causes them to question the FP's commitment to the relationship, such as not texting back, the Borderline can spiral into self doubt, and gut-wrenching feelings of abandonment can kick in. You will probably have experienced this yourself and maybe found that your reaction caused your FP to back out of your life ? This painful situation is compounded by the fact that many Borderlines find they have few friends ,if any, so the loss of the FP is felt even more acutely. It is almost as if the Borderline is addicted to the FP.

## ADDICTIONS

We spoke a little about how substance abuse can act as a risk factor for self-harm in people with BPD in a previous section. Self-harm can also be a form of addiction as the person engaging in self-harming behaviors is drawn towards it more and more on gaining the relief the injury provides

Use of substances significantly impacts and exacerbates the symptoms of BPD. Substance abuse is a type of chemical addiction that refers to addiction involving the use of substances. It is a way to self-medicate or seek relief from pain. The use of substances gives the person a strong feeling of short-term reward known as a "high". Once the effect of the drug or substance starts to die off and the feeling of this high subsides, the drug user is back in their normal life and the circumstances they were in before they felt that good. To achieve the same high and feel just as good as they did before, that person will repeat the use cycle and that creates addiction.

Someone with BPD already struggles with managing their emotions, relationships and triggers. Substance use addiction can become an unhealthy coping mechanism for some people with BPD, if they find that they can use the "feel good" to escape their problems and distresses.

Not everyone with BPD has a substance use addiction, and not everyone with an addiction problem has BPD. We are visiting an overlap between BPD and addiction to view the presentation that can occur in someone with BPD. Both substance abuse and BPD are characterized by impulsivity and destructive behaviors, and mood swings that range from severe depression to periods of intense energy. If you combine the two, the outcome is ten-fold more lethal. People with BPD are already more likely to be impulsive and suicidal to begin with. They become far more prone to self-harm and other reckless behaviors with use of drugs or alcohol.

Many Borderlines,perhaps you included, turn to substances as a means of numbing their intense,negative emotions. It isn't just substances which become an addiction.Some may find they are addicted to shopping which brings a temporary short lived high only to be followed by guilt and remorse.

Putting yourself at risk in dangerous sexual encounters can also become addictive .It can escalate out of control as a greater and greater thrill is sought ,alongside the need to be attractive and "wanted"by someone even in this context.

## RELATIONSHIPS: "PLEASE COME BACK...DON'T COME BACK."

People with BPD generally have a difficult time forming and maintaining relationships. The emotional lability and impulsivity that BPD afflicts upon a person are very difficult to deal with. People with BPD may be needy and dependent on their partner, or feel that their partner isn't there for them enough. When we consider how life has been unkind to people with BPD perhaps growing up in a dysfunctional household, with unpredictable or abusive caregivers, we can sympathize better and understand where their dependency and fears of abandonment and rejection come from.

BPD in relationships can create a lot of conflict and dysfunction, as compared to other relationships. One can even call it an "emotional rollercoaster" because of how rapid the shifts in mood and emotions are. This is the same for both parties. If you are in a relationship with someone who has BPD and are reading this to gain some understanding, you might see your partner experience unpredictable mood shifts and bouts of depression, anxiety, or anger. At times they may love you passionately and need you close by. Other times, they might suddenly withdraw or lash out at you and get upset, question your loyalty, or end the relationship.

Splitting is confusing and tough and a loving partner will try to avoid triggering at all costs. You may ,however have found yourself in a toxic relationship where your partner deliberately provokes splitting . Either way you are torn between feelings of hate and loathing for the partner ,and being desperate not to be left:- not to be abandoned. A tag line often associated with Borderlines is "I hate you/Don't leave me".

Someone with BPD may alternate between feeling secure and loved in the relationship and withdrawing from their partner. Self-sabotage is telling your partner to leave you alone, or threatening to leave them when you feel triggered. You want their love but you find that you are punishing yourself by pushing them away. This kind of reaction is not a response to what has happened between you and your partner, but it is you reacting to what it reminded you of from your past.

The relationship can feel cyclic at times, and the BPD relationship cycle tells us about the pattern or series of highs and lows that can be seen in it.

At stage 1, the relationship begins with passion. You hold your partner in high regard, praise them, give them all your attention and hope or expect them to do the same. You probably,and without realising it, inflate the positives and might feel like they are "the one."

As the relationship progresses to stage 2, you become more sensitive to words and actions that could possibly hold even the slightest hint of negativity. You may fixate on the smallest of things like a late reply to their text or a missed call, and begin to question their motives and interest. This comes from a place of anxiety, a fear of abandonment and low self-worth. The symptoms of BPD will start to flare up and interfere.

At stage 3, the relationship can take on a different tone again. You might start testing out your partner,deliberately push them away or behave unacceptably .You might cause arguments for no reason just to see how willing they are to fight for the relationship.

Stage 4 rolls around and you will start to distance yourself from the love of your life, letting the relationship spiral downward because at that point, you are convinced that they are going to leave you. This is really painful for you. You don't want them to leave, and they don't want to leave you either. When they express confusion, you will hide away your real feelings and pretend that everything is fine.

Stage 5 may be where the relationship ends, especially if your partner isn't aware yet that you are Borderline or just what that means ie this is the playing out of symptoms and not what you really want. Borderlines experience intense mood swings, ranging from sadness at the loss of the relationship to anger against the other person. The fear of abandonment becomes a reality and it fuels your emotional lability.

There may be attempts by them to resolve things but if the relationship is really over, then we're at stage 6, where the Borderline might spiral downward and experience a bout of severe depression. They may give into their thoughts of low self-worth and even resort to reckless behaviors and self-harming to seek distraction and relief.

If the relationship hasn't ended, the cycle may start all over again.

The occurrence of this cycle and its intensity depends on whether or not you are managing your illness by seeking professional help, and if you have other sources of emotional support. The BPD cycle is not a sure thing to happen for people that have or know someone with BPD, nor is it an official symptom of the condition. However it is really very common and even if not officially a symptom ,it is symptomatic.

The idea that people with BPD cannot 'hold down' relationships, however, is a misconception and as a matter of fact, many people with BPD do have healthy and successful relationships, especially if they have been in, or are going through therapy. Because of the intensity of their emotions ,Borderlines can be the most loving, caring empathic and fun partners.

# 6

# "SOMEONE...HELP ME, PLEASE." - DIALECTICAL BEHAVIOR THERAPY

## "I just got diagnosed. What do I do now?"

W e have previously discussed the process of getting a diagnosis, and the role of therapists and psychiatrists. Most importantly, we have made an effort to gain insight into what Borderline Personality Disorder is like, how it manifests and the reasons behind it all, the ways in which it makes things difficult, and even addressed the stigma behind it.

We now come to a learned, growing, and hopeful truth that there is help. By seeking help and finding the right treatment that suits you, whether it's therapy, medication or a combination of both, you will be able to manage your symptoms and have a better quality of life. The pain of living with BPD will not last and you do not have to be alone in finding your way out of its shackles to live the healthy and happy life you deserve.

We will discuss the golden standard treatment for BPD in some depth here.It is a form of talking therapy known as Dialectical Behavior Therapy (DBT). Firstly, what does 'dialectical' even mean? It means two opposite things being true at the same time. According to Marsha Linehan, who developed DBT, dialectical thinking refers to a middle ground between two completely opposite ways of thinking. Instead of trying to pick either the good or bad side, you learn to accept both at the same time, take both views into account and try to unite them for less conflict and more solutions. It's like understanding that the pendulum does swing both sides but it won't stay on either end, it will oscillate to its middle, more stable point. Dialectical thinking helps you accept two truths at the same time, and not one over the other. For example, instead of thinking, *I am trying, but I want to do better* you replace the "but" with an "and" to think *I am trying, AND I want to do better.* Acceptance and change go hand in hand.

Now, what is behavior therapy? Behavior therapy refers to treatment with techniques that help someone change the way they respond to situations. It addresses problematic or unhelpful behaviors and works to reduce them or replace them with more helpful responses.

Dr. Marsha Linehan, a psychologist and researcher, is famous for creating DBT, the most effective form of psychotherapy known for BPD patients. She also developed 'the biosocial theory' which explains that there are three causes of BPD: biological, social, and the interaction between those two factors. Dr. Marsha has opened up about her share of emotional and mental struggles as well as her own diagnosis of BPD. The spark of interest and gain in speed of research in BPD grew tremendously once DBT got coined. That is why DBT is associated so closely with the treatment of BPD, but it can be used as a tool by anyone looking to improve their lives, especially sufferers of any chronic illness.

DBT is designed to cater to those who feel emotions intensely and as a result, face a build-up of stress in their lives. Instead of tackling ways to convert negatives to positives, and bad thoughts into good thoughts, the prime focus of DBT is to help you acknowledge and accept your feelings and behaviors.

DBT is not the only type of talking therapy there is. Additionally, there is a multitude of therapies that are evidence-based treatments for mental illness, as well as counseling or coaching. Those therapies could help with any other,co-morbid,conditions you have such as anxiety or depression.

## HOW DOES THERAPY HELP?

Talking therapy does not work the same way as medication, which is another treatment option that shows a good prognosis for other mental health illnesses that a Borderline may suffer with. Therapy takes more work and time but it is more sustainable in the long run. What you learn about yourself and life in general in therapy sticks with you. It gives you the chance to lay out the map of your mind with the help of your therapist, and figure out how it works. You and your therapist work in collaboration to find solutions, learn new perspectives, and navigate your life using guidance, encouragement and consolation. Your therapist will listen to what you have to say, your thoughts, and your feelings. They have a neutral stance, are supportive and there to help see you through your difficulties. They will get to know about you, your life, and your relationships and help you handle your difficulties, only for your betterment and to pave the way to an improved life. Let's look at some types of therapy before we discuss DBT in complete detail. It should help you understand how therapy works overall.

## Cognitive Behaviour Therapy

By definition, Cognitive Behaviour Therapy is a psycotherapy that revolves around a person's actions and how their thoughts affect them. Its essence is based on the thought that faulty or maladaptive thinking habits give rise to negative beliefs and maladaptive feelings. It suggests that there is a strong relationship between thoughts, behaviors and feelings. It does not emphasize exploring past traumas or emotion regulation so much. DBT branches out from CBT, and it is considered a sub-type while there is still plenty of overlap between the two.

CBT works to break down the unhelpful beliefs followed by unhelpful behaviors. It helps you to learn how to spot when you are slipping into your old bad habits and thinking patterns, and have exit strategies ready. People can learn ways of thinking that serve them and make their life easier. CBT can aid you in developing new habits that will relieve your symptoms.

It works by bringing your focus to the present thoughts and beliefs that are subconsciously dictating the way you respond to situations. You can confront your unhelpful thinking patterns and point out the flaws in them. Once you understand the problem, you can develop healthy coping mechanisms to work around the obstacles. By growing more aware of what thinking your routes your brain is taking, by mapping where you are experiencing potholes or speed bumps, you will feel more in control and reduce the risks of crashing into a negative mood. The goal is to challenge thoughts and ground yourself in reality.

CBT learning tools include:

- Exposure to fears
- Keeping a thought and action diary or journal
- Regular sessions
- Techniques to calm the mind and body

## Addressing unhelpful thoughts

CBT brings your awareness to some unhelpful thinking patterns that are also commonly known as logical fallacies or cognitive distortions. Here are some examples.

*All or Nothing thinking/overgeneralizing*: You start seeing a negative pattern and assuming the worst of things based on one event.

Ask yourself what confirms your belief. What makes you think the way you are thinking is actually confirmed by what's real? Is there any proof?

*Mind reading*: You assume what others are thinking

Say what you feel in clear terms. Adopt effective communication skills like being able to state your likes and dislikes. People cannot read your mind and know what you want without you asking for it or sharing your thoughts. You also cannot assume what others are thinking since you aren't in their head.

*Labeling*: After making a mistake or slipping up, you don't say "I've made a mistake, and I'll do my best to make up for it." but you think you're a "loser" or you're "stupid"

## Interpersonal psychotherapy (IPT)

Interpersonal therapy focuses solely on you and your relationships with other people in your life. It focuses on improving the interpersonal aspect of your life to improve functioning and relieve you from your symptoms. It is especially effective in treating depression ,a problem those with BPD often also have.

IPT is ideal for offering a social support system of sorts as it aims to prevent relationship breakdown. It focuses on particular areas, such as conflict that is acting as the source of your stress, major life changes that are affecting feelings about yourself, grief or loss, and difficulty in maintaining relationships. The goal is to develop a toolkit of strategies to implement when dealing with interpersonal problems to lessen the intensity with which symptoms affect you and to help avoid the breakdown of your relationships.

## HOW DOES DBT WORK?

DBT has been proven to be an effective treatment option for patients with BPD. (Stiglamayr, 2014) It brings together the opposites that are acceptance and change; accepting a negative statement, thought, feeling or action by the therapist and the patient, and following it up with reassurance and figuring out the work needed to gradually switch the negative behaviors into better ones.

The combination of DBT steps and components works in harmony to train the patient to adopt new behaviors that are directed toward the very symptoms they struggle with, namely an unstable sense of self, turbulent interpersonal relationships, emotion dysregulation, fear of abandonment and rejection, and impulsivity. Imagine the stress that someone with BPD has to live with. It is difficult to imagine the weight of the hardship BPD sufferers have to carry because you cannot know what BPD is like unless you have to live it yourself. DBT can take 6 months to one year of treatment, although there isn't a well-defined time constraint for it as many cases of BPD differ and treatment duration may vary, depending on the patient's prognosis.

DBT addresses the symptoms of BPD by equipping the patient with healthy coping skills using different strategies that we will discuss shortly. It has proven to be effective for BPD in reducing risks of suicide, reduced symptoms of depression and anxiety, and lessened days of hospitalization, so it shows promise and good prognosis. (Stiglmayr, 2014)

BPD is characterized by recurring acute periods of intense emotional distress and disturbance. People suffering from BPD can experience rapidly shifting moods and intense bouts of anger as a result of the emotional dysregulation, that is characteristic of the disease. Additionally, patients struggle with identity disturbance and their self-image, forming and maintaining relationships, and controlling impulsive behaviors.

The goal of this behavioral treatment is to guide the clients in learning better adaptive behaviors that can aid in processing and regulating their emotions.

## THE FOUR CORE MODULES OF DBT

### 1. Mindfulness

We discussed some tendencies that BPD patients have such as unstable interpersonal relationships where they can idealize and devalue other people in their life as well as themselves, the tendency to fixate on trivial details of events or the tone of someone they spoke to, and feeling insulted. To address faulty thinking and behavior patterns, the main skill that's taught targets the patient's tendency to act impulsively when emotions have pooled. This is divided into *"what"* skills and *"how"* skills, each set working to help the patient be aware and in the present rather than overthinking the past or the future.

## DBT *"What"* skills

'What' skills enhance mindfulness by helping the person stop, observe and identify what is occupying their mind.

*"Hey, what am I feeling right now? Where is this coming from? Where do I feel it the most in my body?"*

It may be an emotion, thought, physical sensation, memories of the past, or anticipation of the future, a person, a stressor, for example. The aim is for the person to observe, identify, and engage with themselves and attend to their wants internally in order to curb the emotions growing to a size and overtaking their mental capacity, which might result in unwanted, strong reactions.

## DBT *"How"* skills

The 'How' skills are to be practiced alongside the 'what' skills. The way that 'what' skills work to help you pinpoint and name what your mind is occupied with, 'how' skills are another mindfulness tactic.

You approach problems and negative emotions using the 'how' skills without judgment or bias. You choose to say, *"Okay. Let's see what this is about and how we can work it out"* instead of taking a judgemental stance, choosing to think either good, over the top, or bad, unwanted thoughts. We don't choose to see "good" or "bad" thoughts. We use these skills to make peace with our mind and understand that the thoughts we get are simply ours to have, but they do not rule us. We can control how we respond to our feelings.

Instead of drowning in your hurt and feeling it so deep in your heart, letting anger absorb you and suffering at the hands of your symptoms, you learn to regulate and be more present in the moment, without judgment toward yourself or others.

Choosing to be non-judgemental will give you relief, as opposed to holding onto bitterness or stress, which causes you pain. The point is to let go, and let yourself live.

## 2. Emotion regulation

Emotion regulation skills are learned so you can intervene in your own responses, and regulate strong emotions before they can lead to distressing reactions or outbursts. The core feature of BPD is difficulty in regulating emotions. Feelings of anger, depression, frustration, irritability, and anxiety are experienced by those with BPD on an unimaginably large scale.

A core concept in DBT is that the mind can be divided into two parts: the Rational Mind and the Emotional Mind. These form the Wise Mind once they are combined. The Rational mind helps us weigh pros and cons, and pick the option that benefits us the most. The Emotional Mind is the opposite of the Rational Mind. It is not irrational, but it works differently in that it does not rely solely on reason. It engages the person's subconscious thinking and their beliefs, their moods, their true feelings and it results in action from the person's urges or their 'gut instinct'. To do what *feels* right comes from the Emotional Mind.

The Wise Mind results when both emotional and logical thinking are utilized in thinking, planning, communicating and all in all, being. It's like when the heart and brain aren't against each other and there isn't a right or wrong side. It is an unbiased state that allows for truce and fairness between the thoughts and feelings whose conflict is what results in the strong reactions, impulsive decision-making and lack of clarity in the Borderline who is going through the depths of their illness.

Emotion regulation in DBT especially targets the person's black and white thinking to gradually tune it into more flexible, sound thinking. It can help the person with their decision-making and be aware of their thoughts and feelings as they arise. Emotion regulation skills can act as a preventive tool to keep thoughts and strong emotions from hurting yourself or others, and acting impulsively in the heat of the moment.

Someone who regularly struggles with strong emotions to an extent that it disrupts their daily functioning, career, interpersonal relationships, and how they view themselves would undoubtedly benefit from learning this set of skills.

The change that follows acceptance is that of learning. Learning emotion regulation skills will lead to better understanding and the practice of more awareness of your own emotions, the same way someone benefits from driving lessons to learn how to drive.

### 3. Distress tolerance

This module focuses on developing skills to help you manage your emotions in stressful situations in healthy ways. The key is to remove yourself from the distress as safely as possible without causing any harm to you or anyone else. As opposed to something that's just making you uncomfortable, a crisis calls for quick action to protect you from extreme stress-inducing circumstances such as extreme pain that is difficult to alleviate and is overwhelming, or when the Emotional Mind is running on overdrive and there is a strong urge to indulge in unhealthy behaviors for temporary relief.

Distress tolerance skills can come into play when reality gets difficult and things feel out of your control. The most anxiety comes from the feeling of not having any control over your circumstances or the situation unfolding. They also have a key role in intervening when the mind starts to race as impulsivity rises. Distress tolerance skills can dampen the person's urges and save them from engaging in self-harm, addiction, or reacting before thinking, in general.

People around you cannot always reach you and you learn to develop these DBT skills to be there for yourself at your times of difficulty. Developing your distress tolerance skills will do a far better job for you in actually calming down.

DBT skills work a lot with acronyms that summarize some steps to implement to help thinking or behavior.

## TIP skill

This is encouraged when the situation or emotional state is negative or overwhelming, and the quickest way out is needed.

'T' stands for Tipping your temperature with cold water. You can splash water on your face, wash your forearms up and down, use your hand to pat cold water on the back of your neck. This creates a 'diving effect' and your body's blood pressure lowers and your breathing slows to calm you down.

'I' stands for Intense exercise. Get up, clap your hands, do jumping jacks or some quick stretches. Movement engages your body, gets your heart pumping and air flowing through your lungs.

'P' stands for Paced breathing and paired muscle relaxation.

## STOP Skill

**S:** Stop. This is the minute you need to stop for, and minimize stimulation or saying anything you aren't sure of and have not thought through.

**T:** Take a step back. This can be both from your thoughts, or from the other person

**O:** Observe and use your senses to absorb your surroundings, but not draw any conclusions. This is also a part of the mindfulness skills.

**P:** Proceed mindfully.

Other distress tolerance skills include:

Self-soothing, where you bring yourself to engage in positive activities or interests that can take you in the direction opposite from stress. The opposite of stress is to soothe.

There's also Distraction, which is along the same lines as self-soothing in the way that it works to take your mind off the stressful factors and find yourself a place to recuperate.

However, it is very easy to fall into a a trap of avoidance, and retreat to one's comfort zones when using these. That is why these skills should be paired with problem-solving to avoid total avoidance, which can make the stress worse since it won't have been resolved. Otherwise, for the problem that is mentally and emotionally draining and not possible to solve soon, these skills are ideal to employ for coping with the problem while one waits for the right time and place for the problem to be solved.

## 4. Interpersonal effectiveness

The goal of interpersonal effectiveness skills is to help patients gain insight on how their behavior is affecting their relationships and view of themselves. This is followed by learning positive behaviors. You do what's in your interest but you ask for and receive what you want without hurting someone, by maintaining the relationship and also keeping your self-respect. You also become more aware of the difference between when to ask for what you want, and when to establish a boundary and say 'no' to someone.

You especially learn to get out of your own headspace to hear others, give them their wants and needs, validate them, and thus keep these relationships in good health.

No one is a perfect communicator, but every skill takes practice to master. That is why we have strategies and exercises to improve the skill sets DBT equips you with. Here's an example:

## The DEAR man strategy

'D' for Describe: describe what you want in clear, simple and straightforward terms.

'E' for Express: express your feelings instead of bottling them up. Let others know how you truly feel. Other people cannot read your mind, so it is up to you to let them know.

**'A'** for Assert: don't simply tip-toe around what you truly want to say. Speak from your heart and be direct.

**'R'** for Reinforce: tell others you appreciate them for making an effort to meet you in the middle, listen to you and try to give you what you're asking for. Acknowledge other people's efforts.

**'M'** for Mindful: again, don't underestimate the power of mindfulness. It can be easy to lose your focus and spiral into your own thoughts.

**'A'** for Appear: body language is a crucial component of communication. Appear attentive, confident, maintain your posture and eye contact.

**'N'** for Negotiate: you are not the only one with wants and needs. Communication is meant to be a fair game. Be open to negotiate with the other person, and consider their side with an open mind.

Remember these objectives to polish your communication skills as well as to speak with a clear mind and a well thought-out plan.

DBT works excellently as a whole to treat BPD symptoms given that the mental healthcare provider and the patient work together on the core dialectic: *acceptance and change*.

DBT is structured using four main components.

# THE FOUR DBT COMPONENTS

## 1. Skills training group

The skills training group targets the deficit of behavioral skills in patients with BPD with the help of the four main training modules: mindfulness, interpersonal effectiveness, emotion regulation, and distress tolerance. This component is set for the patients in a 'classroom setting', where the skills are taught with relevance to their everyday lives. The group leader instructs and teaches, walking the members through the skills and their applications followed by homework and worksheets.

The group of people meets weekly for a 2 hour session for the duration of 6 months to cover the skill syllabus with the goal of completing the training modules. Group sessions are effective in that it helps everyone who's struggling to feel less alone and more comfortable being in a learning environment with people that share the same struggles.

## 2. Individual psychotherapy

One-on-one DBT therapy helps the patient gain motivation to apply the learned skills to their challenges and the changing events in their life. The therapy sessions are one-hour long and carried out weekly alongside the skills groups.

### 3. Telephone consultation

DBT telephone consultation is an additional form of coaching that is for counselling the patient in the moment when they are in need of it. The patient may phone their therapist outside the formal sessions to get reminders of what they have learned and even have some consolation in crises. Telephone consultation is immensely beneficial in even preventing potentially life endangering situations.

### 4. Therapist consultation team

A DBT consultation team comprises of DBT therapists, counselors or coaches that work together to treat their clients. The team members meet regularly to help each other out and discuss their stress or burnout from their regular line of work.

DBT providers also need support to make sure they can stay motivated and be effective in the work that they do. Those that provide support could also use it in return.

## DRUG THERAPY

Borderline Personality Disorder is a cluster of symptoms that can include identity disturbance, emotional lability, depression, anxiety, impulsivity, intense feelings all in all, and compulsions to self-sabotage.

BPD is mainly treated with psychotherapy, and drug therapy can also be included for the prime treatment of the otherwise debilitating symptoms of BPD. In the exceptional cases of BPD with comorbidities or other health conditions, managing the psychiatric symptoms may be best done by pharmacologic intervention i.e. medication, which can only be prescribed and taken under the supervision of a psychiatrist.

There is no specific class of drugs dedicated to treating Borderline Personality Disorder the way that there are drugs for treating depression or anxiety.

For managing a complex mental illness such as BPD that has an amalgamation of various symptoms, medication is an option to be explored with the help of a GP and psychiatrist. Recent evidence states that anticonvulsant drugs that are used to treat seizures such as *valproate* and *lamotrigine*, and antipsy-chotics such as *olanzapine* and *aripiprazole*, can be effective in treating some symptoms of BPD and their management (Ripoll, 2013).

DBT and medication are necessary to rehabilitate the patient and help them reach a place of stability, where they are secure enough to build stronger coping skills and prevent chances of future harm. Both are important parts of the equation that treats BPD and the other mental health problems the Border-line has.

The diverse individual experiences of symptoms among people with BPD add complications to the management of BPD in the way that there is no single, go-to, foolproof treatment for it. It is the responsibility of mental health professionals to assess each patient fully, taking into account the details of their lifestyle, upbringing, family history and current circumstances, and relationships. Only then can an effective treatment strategy be devised that works in the patient's best interests.

In summary,you should have a treatment plan which is unique to you,formulated by the mental health professionals helping you,in consultation with one another.

# 7

# ALTERNATIVE THERAPIES AND SELF-HELP

## It isn't easy to treat, but it is treatable

As we grow older, our mind and body are challenged all the more. Systems can face error some times, especially when they aren't regularly checked on and maintained, just like cars. We fall ill when any system in our body gets compromised. Like when we catch a cold or get an upset stomach, our body's normal defense processes are disturbed. Unhealthy practices like excessive intake of drugs and alcohol, poor oral hygiene , poor diet and sleep, increased screen time, can take hold.

When you aren't giving your body what it needs to thrive, you are compromising on your health. Your body remembers how it is treated. You know the saying that goes "Treat your body like it's a temple",well, it's true after all.

Lots of people are willing to opt for medication, and as a result, they end up doing quite well. However, it isn't easy for them, because they have to go through the process of trial and error in trying to find the right medication that suits them. Not all medicines work the same way, because everyone is wired differently. We talked about how different experiences of people with BPD can be, and how not everyone suffers the same. On the other hand, some fear the side effects and don't want to be dependent on pills thinking that they will solve their problems. Some cannot even afford medication and regular appointments with a psychiatrist. It isn't wrong to be against taking medication in considering your treatment options. There are multiple other routes you can take to heal and live a better life without medication.

(The following suggestions would not be alternatives to DBT and if you are undergoing or recently finished this treatment, consult with your therapist beforehand)

## FOOD AND SUPPLEMENTS

Nutritional deficiencies can be contributing factors for many diseases, including mental health disorders such as depression, anxiety, bipolar disorder, and schizophrenia.

### Omega 3 Fatty Acids

Research has found a significant link between Omega 3 Fatty Acid deficiency and psychiatric signs and symptoms such as marked impulsivity and aggression. (Bellino & Bozzatello, 2021)

Omega 3 fatty acids have shown to be an effective treatment in people diagnosed with BPD. In a study conducted by Dr Mary Zanarini and Dr Frances Frankenburg, subjects supplemented with 1000 mg of Omega 3 fatty acids daily over the course of 8 weeks turned out to show a notable decrease in symptoms of depression as well as aggressive tendencies. (Zanarini & Frankenburg, 2003)

Here are food items that are excellent sources of Omega 3 fatty acids that you can consider adding to your diet.

- Cold-water fatty fish such as salmon, tuna, and sardines
- Nuts and seeds such as walnuts, chia seeds and flaxseed
- Brussel sprouts and cauliflower
- Plant-derived oils such as canola oil, flaxseed oil, soybean oil

## Vitamins and Minerals

Vitamin B1 deficiency can add to poor self-care and diet, which is one of the contributing factors for development of anxiety and depression, among many other BPD symptoms. Your brain needs these nutrients to convert the sugar in your blood from eating into energy. Did you know your brain's main source of energy is glucose? You've got to eat right to feel better. Vitamins C and D have also been found helpful in managing some symptoms of BPD, alongside the B group.

Besides vitamin B1, vitamin B12, iron, and omega 3 fatty acid deficiencies can cause brain fog. Brain fog can make you feel weighed down, confused, and fatigued. Stay well-nourished to make sure you have all you need to feel good in your body and mind, and to have enough mental energy to heal.

## Magnesium

One of the outstanding properties of magnesium is that it helps your muscles function smoothly, relieving them from tightness, soreness and cramps. It acts as a natural muscle relaxant. Stress and anxiety is a significant cause for muscle stiffness and pain, because your body holds tension in your muscles in a state of stress. Stress activates the fight or flight mode. When you're in fight or flight mode, your muscles contract to get you ready to run or react. When you hold that tension for prolonged periods due to chronic stress or anxiety, and there isn't any threat either, your body's systems can be challenged. In the long run, it can lead to more serious consequences such as high blood pressure and heart disease.

Magnesium benefits the brain. It helps relay signals between the brain and the nervous system through the rest of the body. It makes sure your learning, memory and brain development are up to mark.

An additional key role of magnesium is that it prevents unnecessary activation of nerve cells. You know, there's always constant electrical signals passing between your brain cells.It is when these are interrupted ,reduced or slowed, or when there is over-activity that problems occur.Good sources of this valuable mineral are almonds, spinach and pumpkin seeds. It can be found in cacao and cocoa with many other beneficial vitamins and minerals. If you can't easily get hold of cacao, a healthy treat is dark chocolate with a cocoa content above 70%.

Nutritional psychiatry is a growing field of exploration and it's an alternative worth trying out. Your brain health is incredibly important, as much as your physical health is, if not more. For many people who aren't benefiting from therapy or aren't responding to medication, nutritional intervention can make a significant difference over time. It can also be a valuable supplement to the traditional treatment methods.

## PHYSICAL EXERCISE

Physical exercise regulates your mood and improves your self-esteem on top of the more obvious physical benefits. Exercising ,including yoga involves using your body and coordination, and ,being capable of performing, gives you a positive, empowering spike in confidence. Incorporating physical exercise into your daily routine can seem daunting at first, so feel free to start slow and easy. Take the stairs, go on a brisk walk to take your mind off things, try 5 or 10 minute workout videos on Youtube, do some simple stretches, anything to get yourself moving, your heart pumping and your blood flowing.

Pay attention to the physical sensations to ground yourself and relieve stress.

Physical activity releases endorphins and serotonin, also known as the happy chemicals. It's one of the healthiest alternatives to turn to if medication fails to improve your symptoms. People overlook their diet and exercise, which are two of the key components your body needs at optimal levels in order to thrive. Yet, they're neglected. If you want to start somewhere, start with what you're putting your body through.

Exercise can be therapeutic because it engages the mind, stimulates your brain as well as your body, and fights depression. It goes to show how much of a valuable asset using your own body to recover can be.

With physical exercise, you also learn to tolerate levels of discomfort. It makes for an excellent coping mechanism, and rehabilitates your senses and your brain structure slowly, and surely.

So, counter your negative emotions with positive emotions by doing what actually makes you feel good and sustains your health in the long run.

Yoga is a particularly beneficial activity for Borderlines as it promotes the well-being of body ,mind, and spirit :- an holistic approach to wellness, including mental health. Yoga is an approach to living which is well worth exploring as a means of managing the symptoms of BPD whilst also reaping the physical benefits. You can begin with YouTube videos if you'd prefer not to join a class.Meditation is a key arm of yoga.

## MINDFULNESS AND MEDITATION

Mindfulness is paying attention selectively. It means to engage your mind using relaxing, easy and healthy techniques such as meditation. Although mindfulness isn't all about meditation, the two are closely linked.

To be mindful, you approach your thoughts without judging them or yourself.

When you've found yourself overthinking, have you ever wished for an 'off' button? A button that you can press and it stops your mind from racing? If only it were that easy.

The mind is a wondrous thing. It's full of ideas, memories, thoughts, associations of things with people and of people with things, like the way warm chocolate chip cookies remind you of your compassionate, sweet and down-to-earth close friend, or how sunsets make you feel.

On one hand, it's great for problem-solving and processing information, and it's always so hard at work. One thing that it isn't so great with is pausing and accepting the present for what it is, letting go of the past for what it was, and leaving what isn't in your control for the future and what it holds.

Your mind isn't great at letting you sit down and simply being with what is, instead of fighting and questioning it, or trying to change it. So often, the mind can be caught up in ruminating, brooding, regretting, overthinking, and all that generates a turbulent, messy and confusing clutter of thoughts in the head-space. Mindfulness lets you take a break from this. All you need for achieving mindfulness is to give it a chance, and keep patience, conscious efforts and consistent practice for it.

Mindfulness is gently guiding your focus to, and growing awareness for the present moment continually. Generally, you focus on the sensations you feel in your body in the current moment and tether to them. When the tethers loosen and break, your mind is let go of and free to get distracted, race with new ideas, look for stimulation in its surroundings and new thoughts to think. It scrambles and your thoughts become a void. Mindfulness is an essential tool that brings it back into its place. You don't have to be a slave to your mind and its chatter.

It is important to be consistent in practice, otherwise it won't work well. It's like trying to light a fire using wooden sticks. It can take a while to create a spark and smoke.

The practice of mindfulness and its benefits have been researched. Findings showed lower depression scores in meditators compared to non-meditators. They also showed greater performance in the structural and functional integrity of the brain. (Yang)

Meditation can teach you to recognize harmful or unhealthy thoughts before they can lead to self-destruction. Let's see how it can be practiced.

## Practicing mindfulness

Depending on how you see it, you can be mindful in any activity you're doing. You could be reading, taking a walk, doing the dishes, cooking, tidying your room, or using your phone. You can make a conscious choice to be mindful and present.

Dr Jon Kabat-Zinn coined Mindfulness Based Stress Reduction (MBSR). He started by inviting patients to take out time for self-care in the basement at the hospital where he worked. Decades later, MBSR is taught and implemented worldwide. Kabat-Zinn states that mindfulness is not about tricking the mind. He is of the view that in order to survive as a species and thrive in communities, we need to be aware of who we are, where we are and how we are.

One of Kabat-Zinn's approaches on mindfulness is about being your own friend, finding peace in your own skin, and a place in the realm of simply *being* by using the capacity of awareness that you are born with.

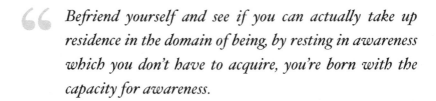

> *Befriend yourself and see if you can actually take up residence in the domain of being, by resting in awareness which you don't have to acquire, you're born with the capacity for awareness.*

— *JON KABAT-ZINN*

Approaching your thoughts non-judgmentally doesn't mean to be completely neutral, but to be aware of your judgment and let go of the restraints you put on your thoughts.

Living in the moment is also a practice of mindfulness. Mindfulness eating is one example, where you eat slowly and focus on the taste and texture of every bite. There is also mindful walking where you pay attention to your surroundings and their details, the clouds in the sky, feeling the wind when it blows, whether you feel hot or cold, and noticing each step you take. All done while you pace your breathing and let your thoughts pass.

With mindfulness, you appreciate and use all five of your senses to ground yourself. Seeing, tasting, hearing, feeling and smelling all engage your mind and body, from the stimuli outside to the brain's processing centers inside. If you are in the moment, you aren't dwelling on the past or worrying about the future.

# Seven key attitudes of mindfulness by Kabat-Zinn

**Non-judging:** Be a witness to the constant stream of your thoughts, wants, judgments and reactions.

**Patience:** Patience branches from wisdom. It shows acceptance of the fact that most things in life will come about and unravel in their own time, and in their own way. You slowly learn to allow it.

**Beginner's Mind:** The first step into any endeavor or area of exploration is catalyzed by curiosity and open-ness. Go into this with open arms and see what comes.

**Trust:** Part of learning any new skill or trying something out is failing a few times. Trust the process and know that it is okay to get back up again.

**Non-Striving:** *Hi. Are you with me? Are you with your-self?* This isn't supposed to tire you. The goal is to watch what comes and unfolds, not to try to make any changes.

**Acceptance:** It isn't about working *hard* at all. We're just watching, seeing things just the way they are. Before making any rash decisions or reacting in haste, just observe. You'll set a plan in life to act calmly.

**Letting Go:** You'll learn that you are holding on tightly to some feelings, thoughts or situations. Sometimes, loosening your grip and letting go of tight ropes is what will give your mind the relief it needs, even when it's hard to let go.

## How to meditate

Here's a simple example:

Put your phone on "Do not disturb" mode, and find a comfortable position.

Check in with yourself and see how you're feeling. Let yourself know that whatever you're feeling is alright. Release tension from your muscles. Lower your shoulders from your ears and unclench your jaw.

Whether you're sitting on a chair or cross-legged, laying down, leaning against the wall or standing, notice the weight of yourself. Your arms and legs. Your hands in your lap or on your sides. Look, you're aware that you are with yourself now.

Start breathing in through the nose and out through the mouth. You can settle at a pace and rhythm you feel relaxed with.

You are cultivating a field of awareness. Listen for the sounds around you. Try separating these sounds, whether it's the fan or ac, people talking in the background, or the sound of people passing by.

Feel the clothes against your skin, how the air feels, how the air is carrying smell and sound that you can take in.

While breathing the same, you will close your eyes and focus on your breath and feel your chest or your stomach rising and falling.

You will notice the stream of your thoughts and feelings and let it flow, just like watching traffic pass by from the pavement, or the clouds as they glide in the sky.

If your mind wanders off into the emotional vortex or random memories and images arise, like how you noticed someone acted odd or they sounded cold when they spoke to you, or how you're tempted to go out drinking again, or how you miss someone you aren't in touch with anymore, let it all pass by and bring your focus back to your breathing.

Stay with your breathing for a while, bringing your mind back to focusing on yourself if it's wandered again.

You can open your eyes when you're ready.

## JOURNALING AND SELF-REFLECTION

Journaling is also known as expressive writing. It is a healthy way of coping with stress as it allows you to articulate your thoughts and feelings without any worry about what someone else thinks of what you're saying. It lets you brainstorm solutions and clarify your thoughts and feelings. Essentially, it gives you a sense of knowing yourself better. For many with Borderline Personality Disorder, journaling can make for a helpful source of relief as it's quite useful in managing intense flare ups of emotions as they come, and in curbing impulses or self-harm urges.

Besides untangling your thoughts and feelings on paper with ink, you can also journal about other areas in life such as goals, plans, or try "gratitude journaling".

With gratitude journaling, you can build on emotional stability and resilience, reduce stress and find more reasons to live a better life.

Journaling helps with sorting out how you feel about situations or events by way of emotional release. You can write about what happened that day, how you felt about it, what bothered you and why. Without any concern for readability or penmanship, you can let your thoughts flow onto paper through ink. It's better to get it all out, than keep it bottled up inside. Journaling your negative experiences can be cathartic in that writing about them lets you have an outlet. Your anger does not stay bubbling up inside you. It can spill out onto the paper.

Here are some prompts, and questions you can ask yourself when you want to write about or dissect the emotional aspects of an event you need to release your pent up feelings:

- What was the situation?
- What did I think or imagined in the situation, and after it?
- How did I feel before, during and after?
- Where did I feel that in my body?
- How does this affect how I see myself, others, and my future?

- What does this change?

You can type your journal, or write with paper and ink. Pick a feasible time to do it, and start incorporating it in your daily routine.

## CBD OIL

Brain centers that control the release of important regulatory hormones are compromised in BPD. The endocannabinoid system (ECS) is present in these brain regions, which produce the body's natural endocannabinoids to regulate its functions and control our thoughts, feelings and responses to the external world.

Many psychiatric disorders can be caused due to hyperactive neurons, which release excessive amounts of neurotransmitters. This can lead to overstimulation, like a message that's being received and spammed so many times, it's causing errors in the system. This overstimulation leads to disturbances in the nervous system as well as in the rest of the body, which causes the psychiatric symptoms.

Endocannabinoids work the opposite way from regular neuronal transmission, meaning they go the opposite direction in which neurotransmitters flow from one neuron to another. This is called *retrograde inhibition*. Therefore, endocannabinoids can mediate and inhibit the overstimulation of neurons by reducing the transfer of some neurotransmitters.

Plant-derived cannabinoids enter your body using CBD, which act the same as the endocannabinoids your body produces. They help alleviate symptoms of BPD i.e. anger, aggressive behavior, impulsivity, and paranoia that are caused by over-excited neurons, by reducing the transfer of neuro-transmitters.

CBD also activates the parts of the brain that release sero-tonin i.e. the "happy chemical." BPD exhibits signs of depres-sion that are likely caused by low serotonin levels. Increased release of serotonin can combat the symptoms of anxiety and depression in Borderlines.

CBD products include hemp oil, which is rich in omega-3 fatty acids. Omega-3 fatty acids are essential for the brain's smooth cognitive functioning due to their anti-inflammatory effects.

Again, BPD does not have a scientific or objective, absolute treatment. Its cluster of symptoms include anxiety, depres-sion, dissociation, splitting, major identity crises and distur-bances, which can best be approached via psychotherapy.

It's well and good to speak to your doctor before starting CBD oil, and seek reliable products rather than just any one that may potentially be unsafe.

Microdosing is defined as taking as small as 5% of a full dose of a psychedelic. Psychedelics are a group of hallucinogenic drugs that bring about changes in perception, mood and cognitive functioning. There is no significant clinical data or research on psychedelic therapy for patients with BPD. It is crucial to consult your doctor if you plan on trying this. There is a total lack of knowledge about psychedelics and micro-dosing at a medical level but, when most treatments fail or haven't been explored first, psychedelic therapy can work on some BPD symptoms when used carefully. Psychedelics have been known to elevate the mood, enhance positive feelings of trust and closeness in relationships, and help patients regain better control over their behaviors.

**Support resources**

- Headspace - Meditation app: Headspace can help you navigate mindfulness with its guided meditation audio tracks.
- Local support groups: Ask your GP, counselor, or therapist about support groups in your area.
- Online support groups. Use your favourite search engine to find these.
- Quora: This is an online platform where an abundance of users sign in to share knowledge that they have about their interests, share their experiences and answer any related questions that other users post.
- Reddit: Similar to Quora, but it includes more interactive discussion forums.
- Facebook groups: There are many FB groups providing Borderlines with a safe place to express themselves,support each other and ask questions

including: Borderline Personality Disorder (EUPD) Support and Chat; Borderline Personality Disorder Support Group ;Borderline Personality Disorder-I Hate You =Don't Leave Me. These are largely private so you have to ask to join.

## Recommended websites:

National Education Alliance for BPD

http://neabpd.org/

DBT Self-Help

https://dbtselfhelp.com/what-is-dbt/

# 8

# LOVING SOMEONE WHEN YOU HAVE BPD & OVERCOMING YOUR FEAR OF ABANDONMENT

## It's worth the effort

Borderline Personality Disorder brings with it numerous challenges daily that are heightened by the impairment in thinking that accompanies any personality disorder. In addition to their intense symptoms, people with BPD also have to pull weight through experiencing mean comments, discrimination, stigma, and isolation. They can be painted as hopeless, hostile, manipulative, or as a danger to themselves and others by people who fail to stop and understand that the behavior and actions are a result of an impairment, that they are not a conscious choice by the sufferer.

## 'YOU ARE CAPABLE OF LOVING OTHERS AND BEING LOVED.'

People forget the positive, unique, and extraordinary features of those with BPD.

When they love, Borderlines do not hold back their passion and affection. They love deeply and are loyal to their partners. Once they have let a positive thing into their life, or someone that they love and care for, they also start to fear the loss of that the way anyone else would. The difference is that their fear of abandonment is so intense, that it can impair them and affect their view of the person. The Borderline begins to adopt defense mechanisms. They can idealize someone they were happy to let in, but then as a subconscious response to the fear of losing them, it can be followed by devaluation of the loved one. And it can go back and forth. Above all, it is worth understanding that those with BPD do not have bad intentions. Their love manifests differently, sometimes in unhealthy ways, but, often, all they need is some understanding and reassurance.

People with BPD know adversity all too well and that *resilience* is one of their strongest traits. They might have struggled with impulsivity, the consequences of giving in to their impulses, drug and alcohol addiction, trauma, self-harm, and daily emotional dysregulation. Most days are battles and wars against their own minds, with their minds working against them. A person without BPD would be unlikely to bear standing in the shoes of someone with BPD for any amount of time.

BPD sufferers have tremendous insight into emotional pain and the ability to recognize and understand those facing turmoil because they've been in the same boat countless times. A significant piece of evidence to back that up is research done on those with BPD compared to a control group without the disorder. It found that people with BPD can tell how someone's feeling by looking at them far better than those without could. This is due to Borderlines' increased sensitivity to how others are feeling, which does impair their relationships but it also lets them gauge how others feel. (Fertuck & Jekal, 2012)

People with BPD are also known to be highly creative individuals. Art holds heart and emotion. One of the core features of observing and making art is the ability to feel emotion. Art, music, writing, and performance allow for healthy stress-releasing tools. People with BPD benefit from art therapy during treatment because it allows them to uncover their emotions and beliefs. It can express the feelings you are dealing with and thus, how your relationships and the people in your life make you feel.

By being able to tell how someone's feeling by looking at them, those with BPD are highly intuitive individuals because they had to learn those skills by growing up in unpredictable surroundings as a child. They are gifted with intuition and awareness for those that aren't doing well, which lets them empathize better instead of overlooking the pain of others.

Above all, people with BPD are more than a diagnosis. They are not their struggles. They are not their problematic and confused thoughts or feelings. They are well-intentioned, loving, compassionate, and caring people. They radiate warmth, ease, purity in being vulnerable, and self-expression. They aren't in the wrong nor are they bad, the main problem they are struggling with is instability. Their sadness and anger are only signs that they are struggling to understand and cope, and that they need help. There are ways to support someone with BPD that can potentially save their lives.

## THE FEAR OF ABANDONMENT

 *"It's like a mother: when the baby is crying,*

*she picks up the baby and she holds the baby tenderly in her arms.*

*Your pain, your anxiety is your baby.*

*You have to take care of it.*

*You have to go back to yourself,*

*to recognize the suffering in you.*

*Embrace the suffering, and you get a relief."*

— *THICH NHAT HANH*

Wanting to feel protected and secure is a basic human need and a quality of the survival instinct. Talking to a professional will help trace the roots of this fear, which is important because, in order to understand a problem and how it is affecting your life, you have to know where it started. If you had a difficult childhood where you grew up in an unstable environment, or weren't loved and cared for by the ones who were responsible for nurturing you, you may fear being abandoned in relationships.

Psychotherapy or group therapy are highly recommended for those struggling with fears of abandonment and rejection.

There is a lot of work you have to do for yourself before you can try to work things out with someone else. BPD is a mental health condition notorious for being characterized unstable relationships with other people accompanied by unstable emotions and a lack of solid sense of self. These features can make dating difficult. Most people with BPD do learn to cope with these features by spending time in talk therapy, learning to name and process their emotions. Remember to catch yourself when you start wondering whether or not your partner is still there for you, or is still interested in seeing things forward. Ask yourself, "Where is this thought coming from?" "Is it possible that this feeling is sprouting from my insecurity?" "Is this a projection of my fear of abandonment?"

It's possible you may have *imagined* being abandoned. Don't accept fantasies of reasons why someone is acting or doing something a certain way or try to figure out what they might be thinking. You cannot conclude where the relationship might be going from someone's body language or something they said that didn't sit right with you.

For starters, accept how real the fear of abandonment is for you, and think about how you react to it. When this fear is triggered, it may be followed by withdrawing from the other person in the relationship to cope with the emotional intensity of it. This is closely aligned with devaluation of the other person you were previously happier with. It can easily lead to a lack of communication.

You cannot think for others, but you can communicate. So as soon as you feel confused or start having doubts, say something. Check your thoughts, write them down. Check what stream your thoughts are flowing in and see what words are coming from them. Try to rule out what thoughts might be real and how they can be backed up with logic or facts. More importantly, listen to what the other person has to say about your point of view and let their reassurance reach you.

## UNDERSTANDING HOW THE BPD MIND WORKS

Here, we discuss a psychological angle that explains some BPD thinking and behaviors. This is to understand some thinking patterns and be aware of them so you can check in with yourself often in trying to understand your emotions.

### Object constancy

Object constancy branches from the established idea of object permanence, which is a cognitive ability or function that babies acquire around age 2 to 3 years old. *Object permanence* lets you understand that people or things are real and continue to exist even when they aren't around to be seen, touched, or heard.

*Object constancy* lets you keep a constant idea or perception of situations, relationships, or people and how you relate to them. People with BPD tend to struggle in this area. For them, when there is distance or conflict, it can shatter their idea of there being a loving relationship at all, and that setbacks do not dissolve the connection that was made.

When they feel like you aren't around or that you are distant, they feel as though you have left them. They struggle to have a stable idea of who they are when they don't have another person to feel loved by. As a result of past trauma, the Borderline has struggled to grow emotionally in a stable way.

For example, a newborn baby starts to cry in distress when the mother lays them down in their crib and leaves the room because they feel as though she has disappeared. When she returns, they can see her again and feel her presence so by then, they are soothed. This is before the baby's *object permanence* skill has developed.

Similarly, the person with BPD lacks object constancy, which leaves them in distress if or when they sense their partner's lack of presence. It can feel like they need constant reminders that the other person won't leave them. Otherwise, they can start to feel as though they aren't cared for anymore, that they will be abandoned.

## DATING

Some people with BPD admit that sometimes they avoid dating in fear of symptoms flaring up. Dating when you aren't aware of your condition is especially distressing. Your perception of yourself and unstable emotions can make you feel worn out all while trying to get along with a new person you intensely like.

In dating, it's best not to compromise on honesty and openness. You can be upfront with your intentions to keep the air clear, and ask the same from them.

The general rule of thumb is to take things slow whenever you start seeing someone. This allows both of you to get to know each other well enough to decide if you want to continue or not. You communicate openly, learn about each other's boundaries, talk about your likes and dislikes, share about your lives and mainly, befriend them.

Your partner is not in control of your disorder. They are not always responsible for how you feel but you can help them understand your mental health condition. You can explain that you sometimes need validation, reassurance, compassion, and really, just an ear that listens and a heart that loves. Their job is not to save you or be your parent.

At the start, it is essential to stick to the boundaries you set. It keeps communication structured. Boundaries can keep the boat from rocking, and the relationship steady. You can ask your partner what their boundaries are and respect them to build a level of trust. What are boundaries in relationships? As the name suggests, you give the person a limited free space to come close to you emotionally with a line drawn somewhere. For example, when you're opening up to them about your past but there is sensitive information that you aren't comfortable with disclosing yet such as triggering details of a traumatic experience, you can communicate that and expect nothing but respect in return. It isn't possible nor realistic to do this in one go. Healthy boundaries are fostered over time and with the support of the other person you are with.

Negative emotions such as jealousy tend to arise in everyone. It is a natural feeling that comes from a place of insecurity. However, combined with your fear of abandonment and rejection, this feeling of jealousy can transcend a healthy threshold onto a tendency to react or speak about it in a way that does not suit the situation. Sometimes, you might find yourself wanting to test them to see if they will leave you, which sounds contradictory. Aren't you afraid of being abandoned? Yes, but at the same time you may worry that they will leave. Insecurity arises in those with BPD much more easily.

In any case, remember to take care of your mental health and stress management. Nothing comes easy. A steady relationship does not come easy, especially when the dynamic is unconventional when a major part of the condition you have to live with makes holding down relationships difficult. It can be easy to get wrapped up in all your challenges and forget self-care. Ask for moral or emotional support from trusted friends or family when you need it. Mostly, talk about and explore topics and interests besides the disorder. You and your partner's lives aren't defined by this diagnosis. Maybe the two of you share a hobby that can help ground you such as painting, video-gaming, cafe hopping, or listening to music.

## YOU DON'T HAVE TO HEAL ALONE

There will be ups and downs, but as long as there is a willingness to learn about BPD, there are ways to nurture and grow healthy relationships and patch up any previous ones.

**Relationship counseling and family therapy**

There's a lot of healthy activities you and your loved one can engage in for mental wellness and to have a healthy relationship foundation, such as taking classes together, doing yoga and going to the gym together.

Additionally, going to group therapy and opening up about struggles and positives together can help set clearer directions to go in for the one with BPD and those learning about BPD with them. Working together allows for there to be a safe space where honesty, willingness to grow and patience are at center.

Seeing a professional that specializes in relationship dynamics, such as a relationship therapist, can help you understand how your disorder affects others in your life. You can break down the details of your relationships whether it's with a partner, family member or friend and learn how each side is contributing in the relationship and how features of your disorder affect the both of you.

In understanding the relationship dynamics, you start to recognize what each person needs. In recognizing other people's needs, you can encourage them to seek help for themselves and take out the time for self-care. You can understand their need for space at times to recuperate and come back to you as well.

You will be able to reflect on your thoughts, actions and behaviors along with support and reassurance during group sessions. This kind of acknowledgement and reflection can give you great opportunities to work through your emotions. It would give the strength to learn about your emotions and having a dial for them so you can control their intensity rather than running away when your feelings get too overwhelming. It helps when there are people to support you through this walk. Sooner,rather than later, you can learn that your feelings won't have a hold on you forever.

Of course, like anyone else in this world, you are not perfect but you have the capacity to learn and improve over time. The people that receive your love and care are lucky to have you. Due to how deeply and intensely you feel, there are chances of hurt in the relationship, but there is loads more capacity to love and be your loved one's FP !

154 · SIENA DA SILVA

**PLEASE LEAVE A REVIEW ON AMAZON IF YOU
FOUND THIS BOOK HELPFUL. JUST ONE
CLICK AND A COUPLE OF MINUTES WILL
HELP OTHERS.
ALWAYS GRATEFUL
AND WISHING YOU HAPPINESS, SIENA.**

# CONCLUSION

Borderline Personality Disorder can cause serious emotional and mental agony for the one suffering from it. It is a mental illness that induces in the sufferer multiple unhealthy and complex tendencies, and its symptoms overlap with other disorders. It is commonly misdiagnosed, which can make it even harder for the person struggling with BPD symptoms to heal.

Borderlines would want others to know that they are just as confused as you are ,and,sometimes, and usually, they are the ones harder on themselves than anyone else. They know something isn't right. They just don't understand why.

It is difficult to move past events and thoughts that have triggered someone with BPD. The spectrum of emotions for someone with BPD is vaster than any, and the dial on the mood meter can change positions quickly in times of distress.

*"Who am I? I don't like myself anymore. Hang on, my hair looks great today. I'm beautiful! Oh, I gained weight again. I can't go out anymore with the way that I look."*

It is self-hatred that can manifest as a multitude of other impairments such as disordered eating, thinking you are overweight when you're not, having a negative self-image, poor self-esteem, unstable identity, or the lack of a sense of self. You wake up wanting to be a new person every day or try something new and drastic. Cutting your hair, deciding to revamp your wardrobe and going on a shopping spree where you end up spending more than you can afford, getting new tattoos and piercings to feel different, and still never feeling truly okay with yourself.

*"He made a new friend today. I guess we won't be spending any more time together. Should I just let go?"*

It is pushing away and pulling in. It's being filled with total adoration for your loved one and then feeling the love you have for them evaporate within the same minute. This can make things confusing and messy. People with BPD search for what they haven't been taught to nurture for themselves in others, such as self-confidence, a sense of identity, validation, and self-love. BPD is being afraid of expressing feelings in fear of being too needy, or suppressing strong emotions until the dam breaks.

BPD can bring your world crashing down on you, and have you wanting to give up on life when in reality, you're just so overwhelmed and cannot find the help you need.

If someone you know or love suffers from BPD, you can do your part in helping by learning about the condition. What it is, how it makes your Borderline think and act, what it puts at stake, what makes it difficult to live with, and how to help someone with it. Search for accessible help options which you can then suggest. If they are on treatment, make sure to check in if they're making their appointments regularly, if they're following the doctor's instructions and taking their medication if it's been prescribed, or if they're attending group therapy sessions. Simply showing up and letting your loved one know that you care for them and want them to feel better can have a positive impact on their recovery.

If you are struggling with BPD, learn to like yourself again. Learn how your world works so you can live in the one around you without clashes. Catch yourself when you feel strongly, lean into the emotions and ask yourself, "Where is this coming from?" Search for any mental health resources you can. Whether it's surfing the web for information, joining online discussion forums to meet others who share the same struggles you have, talking to a trusted friend or loved one and telling them what you feel, or seeing a doctor, counselor, therapist or psychiatrist, find help to feel okay.

BPD is a lot to handle, but it is not a life sentence that is meant to leave you feeling hopeless and helpless. Having BPD is not a choice, it is a struggle, an affliction. But, things can get easier with time and effort. You can learn to live and love just like the new light at dawn at the start of every day brings with it the promise and hope of another chance for things to get better.

# BIBLIOGRAPHY

Bellino, S., & Bozzatello, P. (2021). Efficacy of Polyunsaturated Fatty Acids (PUFAs) on Impulsive Behaviours and Aggressiveness in Psychiatric Disorders. *International Journal of Molecular Sciences*. https://pubmed.ncbi.nlm.nih.gov/33435512/

Fertuck, E.A., & Jekal, A. (2012). Enhanced 'Reading the Mind in the Eyes' in borderline personality disorder compared to healthy controls. *Psychol Med*. https://www.ncbi.nlm.nih.gov/pmc/articles/PMC3427787/

Goodman, M. (2017). Suicide attempts and self-injurious behaviours in adolescent and adult patients with borderline personality disorder. *Personal Mental Health*. https://pubmed.ncbi.nlm.nih.gov/28544496/

Grambal, A. (2016). Quality of life in borderline patients comorbid with anxiety spectrum disorders – a cross-sectional study. *Patient Prefer Adherence*. https://www.ncbi.nlm.nih.gov/pmc/articles/PMC4975144/

Lis, E. (2007). Neuroimaging and genetics of borderline personality disorder: a review. *J Psychiatry Neurosci*. https://www.ncbi.nlm.nih.gov/pmc/articles/PMC1863557/

Oumaya, M. (2008). [Borderline personality disorder, self-mutilation and suicide: literature review]. *Encephale* . https://pubmed.ncbi.nlm.nih.gov/19068333/

Ripoll, L. H. (2013). Psychopharmacologic treatment of borderline personality disorder. *Dialogues Clinical Neuroscience*, 213-224. https://www.ncbi.nlm.nih.gov/pmc/articles/PMC3811092/

Sansone, R. A. (2011). Substance Use Disorders and Borderline Personality. *Innov Clin Neurosci*. https://www.ncbi.nlm.nih.gov/pmc/articles/PMC3196330/

Stiglamayr, C. (2014). Effectiveness of dialectic behavioral therapy in routine outpatient care: the Berlin Borderline Study. *Borderline Personal Disord Emot Dysregul*. https://www.ncbi.nlm.nih.gov/pmc/articles/PMC4579507/

Stiglmayr, C. (2014). Effectiveness of dialectic behavioral therapy in routine outpatient care: the Berlin Borderline Study. https://www.ncbi.nlm.nih.gov/pmc/articles/PMC4579507/

Stoffers-Winterling, J. (2012). Psychological therapies for people with border-line personality disorder. *Cochrane Library*. https://www.cochranelibrary.com/cdsr/doi/10.1002/14651858.CD005652.pub2/full

Yang, C.-C. (2019). Alterations in Brain Structure and Amplitude of Low-frequency after 8 weeks of Mindfulness Meditation Training in Medita-tion-Naïve Subjects. *Scientific Reports*. https://www.nature.com/articles/s41598-019-47470-4

Zanarini, M., & Frankenburg, F. (2003). omega-3 Fatty acid treatment of women with borderline personality disorder: a double-blind, placebo-controlled pilot study. *Am J Psychiatry*. https://pubmed.ncbi.nlm.nih.gov/12505817/

Printed in Great Britain
by Amazon